GRAMMAR FOR GREAT WRITING

C

SERIES CONSULTANT
KEITH S. FOLSE

LIDA BAKER

ROBYN BRINKS LOCKWOOD

KRISTIN DONNALLEY SHERMAN

Australia • Brazil • Mexico • Singapore • United Kingdom • United States

Grammar for Great Writing:
***Student Book C,* First Edition**
Lida Baker • Robyn Brinks Lockwood • Kristin Donnalley Sherman

Publisher: Sherrise Roehr

Executive Editor: Laura Le Dréan

Senior Development Editor: Jennifer Bixby

Media Researcher: Leila Hishmeh

Senior Technology Product Manager: Scott Rule

Director of Global Marketing: Ian Martin

Product Marketing Manager: Dalia Bravo

Sr. Director, ELT & World Languages: Michael Burggren

Production Manager: Daisy Sosa

Content Project Manager: Beth Houston

Senior Print Buyer: Mary Beth Hennebury

Composition: SPI-Global

Cover/Text Design: Brenda Carmichael

Art Director: Brenda Carmichael

Cover Image: ©Kacper Kowalski/Panos Pictures

A view over a forest lake in Kashubia, Poland, reveals changing fall colors.

For product information and technology assistance, contact us at
Cengage Learning Customer & Sales Support, cengage.com/contact
For permission to use material from this text or product,
submit all requests online at **cengage.com/permissions**
Further permissions questions can be emailed to
permissionrequest@cengage.com

Student Edition:
ISBN: 978-1-337-11861-3

National Geographic Learning
20 Channel Center Street
Boston, MA 02210
USA

National Geographic Learning, a Cengage Learning Company, has a mission to bring the world to the classroom and the classroom to life. With our English language programs, students learn about their world by experiencing it. Through our partnerships with National Geographic and TED, they develop the language and skills they need to be successful global citizens and leaders.

Locate your local office at **international.cengage.com/region**

Visit National Geographic Learning online at **NGL.cengage.com/ELT**
Visit our corporate website at **www.cengage.com**

Printed in the United States of America
Print Number: 02 Print Year: 2017

Contents

Scope and Sequence

Unit	Common Errors	Vocabulary in Academic Writing	Kinds of Writing
1 **Nouns and Noun Phrases**	1.1 Does a singular count noun have a determiner? 1.2 Does a count noun have a plural ending? 1.3 Is the noun plural or not? 1.4 Does the noun need an article or not? 1.5 Do you need *much* or *a great deal of*?	*Nouns from the Academic Word List* attitude, bias, colleague, device, distinction, enforcement, incidence, outcome, procedure, publication	Classification: *Measuring Earthquakes* Problem–Solution: *Job Satisfaction of Hospital Doctors*
2 **Writing about the Past**	2.1 Do you need simple past or simple present? 2.2 Do you need verb + *-ing*? 2.3 Do you need simple past or past progressive? 2.4 Do you need simple past or past perfect?	*Verbs Frequently Used in Past Progressive* become, do, get, have, look, make, take, try, use, work	Descriptive: *Guernica* Narrative: *The 1989 World Series*
3 **Using the Present Perfect**	3.1 Do you need present perfect or simple present? 3.2 Do you need present perfect or simple past?	*Verbs Frequently Used in Present Perfect* be, become, come, find, have, lead, make, see, show, take	Descriptive: *Flipped Classrooms* Narrative: *A Brief History of Flight*
4 **Using Word Forms**	4.1 Is the word form correct? 4.2 Do you have the correct suffix?	*Frequently Used Words with Common Suffixes* community, consistent, creativity, emphasize, finally, individual, mechanism, positive, section, strengthen	Cause–Effect: *The Dangers of Sitting* Summary–Response: *Functional Textiles*
5 **Writing with Prepositions**	5.1 Which preposition is correct? 5.2 Do you have a noun form after the preposition? 5.3 Does the main verb of the sentence agree with the subject?	*Frequently Used Preposition Combinations* associated with, consistent with, difference between, due to, lack of, need for, reason for, responsible for, support for, used to	Process: *Your Immune System* Problem–Solution: *How New York City Faced a Challenge*
6 **Using Modals**	6.1 Is the form of the modal correct? 6.2 Do you need a modal to hedge? 6.3 Do you use *I think* or *maybe* for hedging?	*Frequently Used Modal + Verb Combinations* can help, cannot be, could lead, may be, may need, may result, might have, must be received, should be taken, would have been	Cause–Effect: *Warning Labels on Sugar-Sweetened Drinks* Advantages–Disadvantages: *Driverless Cars*
7 **Using Gerunds and Infinitives**	7.1 Do you need a gerund as the subject? 7.2 Does the verb agree with the gerund subject? 7.3 Is *to* a preposition or part of an infinitive? 7.4 Do you have *by* + gerund?	*Frequently Used Infinitives and Gerunds* becoming, being, having, making, using, to be, to do, to have, to make, to use	Descriptive: *Phobias* Cause–Effect: *Treating Acne*

Unit	Common Errors	Vocabulary in Academic Writing	Kinds of Writing
8 **Using the Passive Voice**	8.1 Do you use the correct form of the verb? 8.2 Do you include a form of *be* in the passive voice? 8.3 Do you need passive or active voice?	*Frequently Used Passive Verb Forms* can be seen, can be used, has been made, have been found, is known, is needed, was based, was conducted, were asked, were reported	Summary: *Our Brains Are Designed to Do Good* Summary: *Media Habits of Students*
9 **Writing with Participial Adjectives**	9.1 Do you need a present or past participle? 9.2 Do you have the correct participial form?	*Frequently Used Participial Adjectives* developing, existing, following, growing, interesting, concerned, gifted, increased, involved, limited	Opinion: *The American Dream* Summary: *Millennials and Marriage*
10 **Adjective Clauses and Reduced Clauses**	10.1 Do you need a subject relative pronoun? 10.2 Do you have the correct relative pronoun? 10.3 Do you repeat the subject or object pronoun? 10.4 Is the subject adjective clause reduced correctly?	*Nouns That Frequently Precede Adjective Clauses with* That activity, approach, area, element, idea, indication, issue, option, organization, result	Cause–Effect: *Ebola* Narrative: *Helen Keller*
11 **Adverb Clauses and Reduced Clauses**	11.1 Do you have the correct subordinating conjunction? 11.2 Do you have a subordinating conjunction? 11.3 Is the punctuation correct? 11.4 Is the clause reduced correctly?	*Words from the Academic Word List* confirmed, decades, eliminate, empirical, equipment, isolated, mode, somewhat, successive, transmission	Descriptive: *Dinesh Patel* Descriptive: *The National Oceanic and Atmospheric Administration (NOAA)*
12 **Writing with Noun Clauses**	12.1 Do you need question or statement word order? 12.2 Do you need *that* or *what*? 12.3 Do the subject and verb agree?	*Frequently Used Reporting Verbs* argue, demonstrate, deny, describe, find, observe, propose, report, show, suggest	Cause–Effect: *Body Size in Sports* Reaction–Response: *Village Dogs*
13 **Writing with Sentence Variety**	13.1 Do you have a complete sentence or a fragment? 13.2 Is there a conjunction? 13.3 Does your sentence need a comma?	*Words from the Academic Word List* advocate, ambiguous, eliminate, fluctuations, infrastructure, intervention, priority, random, restore, voluntary	Comparison: *Two Smart Birds* Comparison: *Neanderthals versus Modern Humans*
14 **Using the Conditional**	14.1 Is the verb form correct for future real conditional? 14.2 Is the verb form correct for present or future unreal conditional? 14.3 Is the verb form correct for past unreal conditional?	*Words from the Academic Word List* anticipated, ceases, coincide, device, erosion, military, rigid, route, undergo, violation	Cause–Effect: *From Garbage to Energy* Cause–Effect: *Save the Bats*
15 **Writing with Connectors**	15.1 Do you need a connector? 15.2 Is the connector correct? 15.3 Is a comma needed? 15.4 Do you have too many connectors?	*Words from the Academic Word List* appreciation, controversy, crucial, denote, diminished, eventually, format, portion, radical, widespread	Comparison: *Print or Electronic Books* Descriptive: *Monaco*

Overview

ABOUT THE *GRAMMAR FOR GREAT WRITING* SERIES

Grammar for Great Writing is a three-book series that helps students with the specific grammar they actually need to strengthen their academic writing. Activities feature academic vocabulary and content, providing clear models for good academic writing. Ideal for the grammar component of a writing and grammar class, *Grammar for Great Writing* may be used as a companion to the *Great Writing* series or in conjunction with any academic writing textbook.

This series consists of three levels: A, B, and C.

Book A is for low intermediate students and is designed to complement the writing and grammar found in *Great Writing 2*.

Book B is for intermediate students and is designed to complement the writing and grammar found in *Great Writing 3*.

Book C is for upper intermediate to advanced students and is designed to complement the writing and grammar found in *Great Writing 4*.

THE RESEARCH BEHIND THIS SERIES

One of the most important differences between *Grammar for Great Writing* and more traditional grammar series is the research base that informed our grammar choices as we developed this series. A traditional grammar series starts with a list of pre-determined grammar points that will be covered, and then exercises are developed for those grammar points. For *Grammar for Great Writing*, however, we started by reviewing academic writing by both nonnative and native students. We looked at ESL and EFL student writing to identify the most common grammar challenges. At the same time, we looked at papers by students in university classes to identify grammatical structures that are common in academic writing but not sufficiently used in our students' writing.

The resulting grammar syllabus is based on actual student needs, not a pre-determined list of grammar points. All the grammatical structures included in this series meet at least one of these two criteria: (1) nonnative writers make errors using the structure, or (2) nonnative writers tend to avoid using the structure.

The material taught in all three books is corpus-informed, using a variety of corpora or corpus-based resources, including the Academic Word List (Coxhead, 2000), the Corpus of Contemporary English (Davies, 2008–), the Michigan Corpus of Upper-Level Student Papers (Ädel & Römer, 2012), student papers from our own courses, as well as empirical research studies of nonnative student writing. Because vocabulary is such an integral part of good academic writing, we have also included a corpus-informed vocabulary section, Academic Vocabulary, in each unit.

ORGANIZATION

Each of the three books in this series consists of 15 units, and each unit focuses solidly on one area of grammar that causes problems for ESL and EFL writers. These 45 grammar points have been selected based on input from experienced English language teachers and student writers. Although many grammar points appear in only one book, others are so important that they appear in more than one book. Students work with the grammar point in increasingly more complex sentences and rhetorical modes as they progress through the different levels of the series.

The units have been carefully designed so that they may be taught in any order. In fact, it is possible to skip units if teachers believe that a particular grammar point is not problematic for their students. In other words, teachers should review the Scope and Sequence, which calls out the common student errors addressed in each unit, and carefully choose which of the 15 grammar topics to present and in which order.

CONTENTS OF A UNIT

Each of the six sections in a unit contains presentation and practice. Although each unit has a specific grammatical focus, the following sections appear in every unit:

What Do You Know?

This opening activity is designed to grab the students' attention and help them assess their understanding of the grammar point. *What Do You Know* has two parts. First, students are directed to look at the unit opening photo and think about how it is related to the topic of the paragraph. They discuss two questions related to the photo that are designed to elicit use of the target grammar. Then students read a paragraph that has two common errors in it. The paragraph has a clear rhetorical style. Students work together to find the grammar errors and explain the corrections.

Grammar Forms

Clear charts present and explain the form of the unit's grammar focus. Follow-up activities focus students' attention on the grammar form.

Common Uses

How the grammar is used in writing is a unique part of the series. The common use charts explain how the grammar point is actually used in academic writing. A follow-up activity provides practice.

Common Errors

Here students are presented with a series of two to five of the most common errors that student writers typically make with the unit grammar point. The focus is on errors found in academic writing, and each error chart is followed by an activity.

Academic Vocabulary

Academic vocabulary is a unique feature of this series. Using corpus and frequency data, we have identified vocabulary that most naturally combines with the grammar focus of the unit. The *Vocabulary in Academic Writing* activity presents items from a broad range of academic subject areas.

Put It Together

The *Review Quiz* gives teachers a chance to quickly check how much students have learned about forming and using the grammar point. In this short activity of only eight items, students answer five multiple-choice questions and then identify and correct errors in three items.

In *Building Greater Sentences*, students combine three or more short sentences into one coherent sentence that uses the target grammar structure.

Steps to Composing is an engaging and interactive activity in which students read a paragraph consisting of 8 to 12 sentences. The paragraph models a specific rhetorical style. While none of the sentences contain outright errors, the writing can be improved. To this end, there are 10 steps that instruct the student in how to improve the sentences. Most of the time the instructions are very specific (for example, combine sentences 2 and 3 with the word *because*). Other times they are intentionally more open in order to challenge the student (for example: add a descriptive adjective to the sentence).

Finally, *Original Writing* consists of a writing assignment connected to the grammar topic, focusing on a specific rhetorical style of writing. There are three example sentences to give the student ideas for a topic. The amount of writing that is required will depend on the student, the teacher, and the objectives for the course.

Acknowledgements

I am grateful to the many people who have worked so hard on the development and production of *Grammar for Great Writing*, including Laura Le Dréan, Jennifer Bixby, and Eve Einselen Yu of National Geographic Learning, authors Lida Baker, Robyn Brinks Lockwood, and Kristin Donnalley Sherman, and contributing editor Pat O'Neill. Ultimately, everyone's ideas and feedback have been instrumental in the design of this work.

I would also like to acknowledge the input from the thousands of ESL and EFL students that I have taught throughout my teaching career. *Grammar for Great Writing* is the result of many years of teaching academic writing to students all over the world. This series is very much based on learner needs, particularly grammar problems that I have seen students struggle with as they are trying to improve their academic writing in English. These classroom experiences have been instrumental in shaping which grammar is covered as well as how it is presented and practiced.

Finally, many thanks to the following reviewers who offered important ideas and helpful suggestions that shaped the *Grammar for Great Writing* series:

Nancy Boyer, Golden West College, California

Tony Carnerie, University of California, San Diego Language Institute, California

Angela Cox, Spring International Language Center, Arkansas

Luke Daly, Harold Washington College, Illinois

Rachel Dictor, DePaul University English Language Academy, Illinois

Ian Dreilinger, Center for Multilingual Multicultural Studies, Florida

Edward Feighny, Houston Community College, Texas

Timothy Fojtik, Concordia University Wisconsin, Wisconsin

Janile Hill, DePaul University English Language Academy, Illinois

Elizabeth Kelley, University of California, San Diego Language Institute, California

Toby Killcreas, Auburn University at Montgomery, Alabama

Lisa Kovacs, University of California, San Diego Language Institute, California

Maria Lerma, Orange Coast College, California

Wendy McBride, University of Arkansas, Spring International Language Center, Arkansas

Kathy Najafi, Houston Community College, Texas

Anne Politz, Drexel University, Pennsylvania

Wendy Ramer, Broward Community College, Florida

Helen Roland, Miami Dade College, Florida

Kody Salzburn, Auburn University at Montgomery, Alabama

Gail Schwartz, University of California, Irvine, California

Karen Shock, Savannah College of Art and Design, Georgia

Adriana Treadway, Spring International Language Center, Arkansas

Anne McGee Tyoan, Savannah College of Art and Design, Georgia

—Keith S. Folse

Series Consultant

Credits

Photo Credits

Cover: Kacper Kowalski/Panos Pictures.

02–03 Peter Essick/Aurora Photos, **14** (t) Roger Bacon/REUTERS/Alamy Stock Photo, **16** (b) Andresr/ShutterStock.com, **18–19** Bruce Bennett/Getty Images News/Getty Images, **27** (bRAUL TOUZON/National Geographic Creative, **31** (t) Ferrantraite/E+/Getty Images, **34–35** TODD ANDERSON/The New York Times/Redux Pictures, **43** (t) Songquan Deng/ShutterStock.com, **46–47** Brooks Kraft/Corbis News/Getty Images, **55** (t) Yvonne Navalaney/ShutterStock.com, **58–59** KARSTEN SCHNEIDER/SCIENCE PHOTO LIBRARY, **61** (b) NunyaCarley/iStock/Getty Images, **70** (t) Roman Korotkov/Shutterstock.com, **72** (b) New York Daily News Archive/Getty Images, **74–75** Robert Clark/National Geographic Creative, **86** (t) JAMES L. STANFIELD/National Geographic Creative, **90–91** LYNN JOHNSON/National Geographic Creative, **100** (b) DESIGN PICS INC/National Geographic Creative, **103** (t) Photographee.eu/Shutterstock.com, **106–107** MAGGIE STEBER/National Geographic Creative, **113** (b) JAUBERT French Collection/Alamy Stock Photo, **117** (t) Attila JANDI/Shutterstock.com, **120–121** H. Armstrong Roberts/ClassicStock/Getty Images, **123** (b) ROY TOFT/National Geographic Creative, **129** (t) NASA/Getty Images News/Getty Images, **132–133** Daniel Berehulak/The New York Times/Redux, **145** (t) Anibal Trejo/ShutterStock.com, **148–149** Doug Benc/Getty Images Sport/Getty Images, **152** (bMARESA PRYOR/National Geographic Creative, **161** (t) Bartosz Hadyniak/E+/Getty Images, **164–165** Adam Pretty/Getty Images Sport/Getty Images, **175** (t) WINFIELD PARKS/National Geographic Creative, **178–179** Tui de Roy/Minden Pictures, **191** (t) MICHAEL NICHOLS/National Geographic Creative, **194–195** ROBB KENDRICK/National Geographic Creative, **205** (t) Axente Vlad/Shutterstock.com, **208–209** Yunus Kaymaz/Anadolu Agency/Getty Images, **221** (t) Fabio Lamanna/Shutterstock.com.

References

Biber, D., Leech, G. & Conrad, S. (1999). *Longman grammar of spoken and written English.* New York: Longman.

Coxhead, A. (2000). The academic word list. Retrieved from http://www.victoria.ac.nz/lals/resources/academicwordlist/

Davies, M. (2008–). *The corpus of contemporary American English: 520 million words, 1990–present.* Available at http://corpus.byu.edu/coca/

Flowerdew, J. (Ed.). (2002). *Academic discourse.* New York: Longman.

Larsen-Freeman, D. & Celce-Murcia, M. (2016). *The grammar book: Form, meaning, and use for English language teachers,* (3rd ed.). Boston: National Geographic Learning/Cengage Learning.

Reilly, N. (2013). *A comparative analysis of present and past participial adjectives and their collocations in the Corpus of Contemporary American English (COCA)* (Master's thesis). University of Central Florida, Orlando, Florida.

Museum visitors in Kobe, Japan, walk through a simulated disaster zone showing the devastation of the Great Hanshin-Awaji earthquake of 1995.

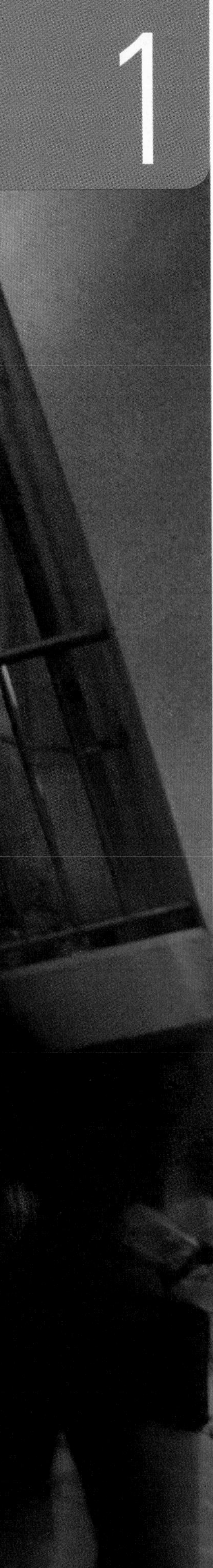

1

Nouns and Noun Phrases

WHAT DO YOU KNOW?

DISCUSS Look at the photo and read the caption. Discuss the questions.

1. What can people learn by visiting this museum exhibit?
2. What do you know about how earthquakes are measured?

FIND THE ERRORS This paragraph contains two errors with nouns and their determiners, such as articles or quantifiers. Find the errors and correct them. Explain your corrections to a partner.

CLASSIFICATION PARAGRAPH

Measuring Earthquakes

[1] To many, earthquakes are one of the worst natural disasters because they can cause many injuries and a great deal of property damage with no warning. [2] Earthquake's strength is determined by measuring two things: magnitude and intensity. [3] Magnitude is the size of an earthquake. [4] An earthquake's magnitude is measured using the Richter scale and is expressed in whole numbers with decimal fractions. [5] For example, a 5.1 magnitude is considered a moderate quake. [6] The Richter scale does not measure how many damage occurs. [7] The intensity, on the other hand, is measured using the Modified Mercalli Intensity Scale (MI). [8] This scale consists of 12 levels of intensity. [9] The MI scale uses Roman numerals. [10] A VII earthquake on the MI scale suggests that ordinary buildings have sustained moderate damage while poorly built structures are likely to be severely damaged. [11] A measure of VIII indicates that chimneys, columns, monuments, and walls will probably fall. [12] Using both scales is the best way to determine the severity of an earthquake.

Grammar Forms

1.1 Count Nouns

Count nouns name things that you can count. They can be singular or plural. A count noun is often preceded by a determiner, which gives additional information to the reader. Determiners include articles (*a, an, the*), quantifiers (*many, a few, several*), and other such words or phrases.

(Determiner) + Count Noun	Example
a / an + singular count noun	**An earthquake** is one of the most destructive natural disasters.
the + singular count noun	**The earthquake** in California in 1906 nearly destroyed San Francisco.
Ø + plural count noun	**Earthquakes** are unpredictable and can strike with enough force to bring buildings down.
the + plural count noun	Three of **the earthquakes** with the highest death tolls took place in China.
many / a few / several + plural count noun	**Many people** were injured in the Artux-Jiashi area of China during an earthquake in 1996.
a large number of + plural count noun	In recent years, fracking has caused **a large number of earthquakes** in Oklahoma.

Notes
1. A determiner is a word placed in front of a noun to help identify it. Examples include *a, an, the, some, my, your, his, her, its, our, their.*
2. To make a noun plural, add *-s* or *-es* (*building**s**, earthquake**s**, wind**s**, beach**es***). If the noun ends in *-y*, change the *-y* to *-i* and add *-es* (*injur**ies**, propert**ies***).
3. Some nouns are irregular. To make irregular nouns plural, there are other spelling changes:
   - change vowel sounds or add a different ending (*m**ou**se. m**i**ce; t**oo**th, t**ee**th; person, people*)
   - change a final *-f* to *-v* and add *-es* (*wol**f**, wol**ves**; kni**fe**, kni**ves***)
   - keep the same spelling as the singular form (*deer, sheep*)

1.2 Non-count Nouns

Non-count nouns name things that cannot be counted (e.g., *advice, information, homework, research*). They do not have a plural form.

(Determiner) + Non-Count Noun	Example
Ø + non-count noun	**Information** on earthquake **safety** can be found on government Web sites.

1.2	Non-count Nouns (Continued)
the + noun-count noun	**The information** on the state website is very useful.
much + non-count noun	Natural disasters do not often allow **much time** for people to prepare.
a great deal of + non-count noun	In order to predict earthquakes, scientists still need to do **a great deal of research**.

1.3 Noun Phrases

Noun phrases are very common in academic writing. A noun phrase is made up of a core noun and other words. Noun phrases often follow one of six patterns.

Structure	Example
1. (determiner) + (adjective) + noun	In the United States, **the government** plays **a significant role** in **education**.
2. noun + noun	**Research grants** are sometimes a viable option for students to fund their **graduate education**.
3. noun + noun + noun	**Student success rates** in online programs are increasing and may eventually rival those of students in traditional courses.
4. noun + noun + noun + noun	**University scholarship application instructions** are usually easy to find, but they can be hard to follow.
5. noun + prepositional phrase(s)	**The increase** in computer science courses is a result of the growing number of engineering students.
6. noun + adjective clause	**Coursework** that can be done online is becoming increasingly common. **Many students** who have young children at home prefer online course options.

Notes

1. In academic writing, it is common for a noun to be followed by one or more prepositional phrases.
2. In academic writing, noun + noun combinations are common, but their meanings are not always obvious.
   Examples:
   a. a computer analysis = an analysis done with a computer
   b. a computer manual = a manual for a computer
   c. a computer programmer = a programmer of computers
3. In any noun + noun combination, note that the last noun is the only noun that can be plural.
   Examples:
   a. two computer problems (not: two computers problems)
   b. five chemistry lab reports (not: five chemistry labs reports)
4. Proper nouns are capitalized: Saudi Arabia, a country; Toyota, a car.

ACTIVITY 1

For each sentence, fill in the blank with the correct determiner and noun combination. Change the noun form if necessary.

1. Because California experiences ______________________ (*many / much, earthquake*) every year, residents are aware of the possible consequences.
2. Earthquakes can cause so ______________________ (*many / much, damage*) to a city's infrastructure that major rebuilding may be necessary.
3. Because this type of natural disaster is so unpredictable, some people have ______________________ (*a great deal of / a large number, fear*) about earthquakes.
4. Scientists are working to predict ______________________ (*a / the / Ø, likelihood*) of an earthquake happening.
5. People in earthquake-prone areas need to design buildings that will not be damaged when there is ______________________ (*an / the / Ø, earthquake*).
6. Because the consequences of earthquakes can be catastrophic, many research studies have been conducted and ______________________ (*much / many, building*) are now designed to withstand earthquakes.

ACTIVITY 2

Read the following sentences. Underline the noun phrases. The number in parentheses indicates how many noun phrases are in the sentence.

1. Dolores Huerta, who is an American labor leader and a civil rights activist, taught in California before becoming a labor organizer. (3)
2. The GED is a high school diploma equivalency exam comprised of five sections: social studies, science, reading, writing, and mathematics. (4)
3. In Ecuador, many types of fruit are harvested and exported to other countries in Asia, Africa, and the European Union. (3)
4. Although the cancer mortality rate has been decreasing, a person's environment and lifestyle can increase the risk. (3)
5. The complicated tax codes in the United States are revised every year by the Internal Revenue Service. (3)
6. When companies undergo restructuring, hiring financial and legal advisors is a common practice to help with transactions and negotiations. (2)

Common Uses

1.4 Using Determiners

Determiners are used before nouns:

1. to let readers know whether the noun is general or specific Singular count nouns must have an article (*a, an, the*) or other determiner. **a.** *A* and *an* are used before singular count nouns that are not specific or are being mentioned for the first time. **b.** Use *the* when you are writing about something specific. **c.** Use *the* when you are mentioning something for the second time.	**A business** needs to have good customer service to succeed. (general) **The business** went bankrupt partly because their customer service was terrible. (specific) Insufficient understanding of diseases can have **a catastrophic effect** on society. **The catastrophic effect** of **the new laws** can only be stopped by government intervention. All students must pass **an exam** to move to the next level. **The exam** takes place three times a year.
2. to make writing more formal by using determiners such as: **a.** *a great deal of* before non-count nouns **b.** *a large number of* before count nouns	*Spoken:* Serious researchers review **a lot of information** before attempting to conduct an experiment. *Written:* Serious researchers review **a great deal of information** before attempting to conduct an experiment. *Spoken:* The university offers **a lot of courses**. *Written:* The university offers **a large number of courses**.

1.5 Using Noun Phrases in Writing

Academic writing often has longer, more complex noun phrases. Some ways writers create these noun phrases are by:

1. using a noun instead of a verb	• *Spoken* (verb): The wind **destroyed** many buildings and they will cost thousands to repair. • *Written* (noun): The wind **destruction** will cost thousands to repair.
2. including as much information as possible in fewer words to be more precise and succinct	• *Spoken*: These scientists study the **patterns** that **birds** use when they **migrate**. • *Written*: These scientists study **bird migration patterns**.

Note
Many nouns with related verb forms end in *-tion* (*destroy, destruction; instruct, instruction*). See Unit 4, Using Word Forms.

ACTIVITY 3

For each sentence, unscramble the words in parentheses to complete the sentence with the correct noun phrase. More than one answer may be possible.

1. Even many decades later, ______________________ (*ideas / psychology / Freud's / about*) are still being studied.

2. Not enough funding is available; therefore, ______________________ (*residents / many / nursing / in / homes*) do not get the treatment they require.

3. During John F. Kennedy's presidency, ______________________ (*of / one / promises / the / made / he / that*) was to end segregation. It was Lyndon B. Johnson who carried out Kennedy's promise.

4. ______________________ (*steady / the / increase / sales / in*) resulted directly from the company's investment in training for its employees.

5. ______________________ (*customer / the / of / the / survey / results / latest*) showed a decline in passenger satisfaction with airline service.

6. Unfortunately, ______________________ (*language / teaching / foreign*) in ______________________ (*U.S. / most / schools*) is often limited to grammar.

7. In the study, participants were not given ______________________ (*time / great / a / of / deal*) to complete the tasks.

8. Each winter, ______________________ (*whales / number / large / humpback / of / a*) return to ______________________ (*island / Maui / of / the / Hawaiian*) to mate or give birth.

9. ______________________ (*for / problem / the / one / characters / common*) in the novel is their inability to cope with the inevitability of change.

10. The poor economy is one reason ______________________ (*education / in / the / post-secondary / enrollment*) decreased last year.

11. ______________________ (*medicine / field / of / the*) has endured much criticism as universities developed academic programs for medical students.

12. ______________________ (*oil / costs / production*) vary based on where the oil is and what taxes are placed on profits.

Common Errors

Common Error 1.1 Does a singular count noun have a determiner?

Some English scholars agree that *War and Peace* is ^a great literary novel because Tolstoy used both primary and secondary sources.

REMEMBER: Do not use a singular count noun without an article or other determiner.

Common Error 1.2 Does a count noun have a plural ending?

Many ~~reader~~ readers have tried to determine the exact number of real people either named or referred to in *War and Peace*.

REMEMBER: Make sure the noun after *many* is plural.

ACTIVITY 4 **Common Error 1.1 and 1.2**

For each sentence, underline the correct answer in parentheses. Choose Ø if no determiner is needed.

1. Biology is the study of life. A biologist studies (*a / the / Ø*) living organism, its structure, and the way it grows.
2. There is no clear cause for (*a / the / Ø*) death of William Shakespeare; however, he made a will, so it is likely he knew death was imminent.
3. According to many research (*study / studies*), pet owners are generally happy with their lives.
4. California joined the United States in 1850 and is home to Los Angeles, (*a / the / Ø*) county with the country's largest population.
5. According to the Centers for Disease Control and Prevention, (*a / the / Ø*) spread of (*a / the / Ø*) germs can be minimized if people use (*a / the / Ø*) tissue to block a sneeze.
6. Chemical engineers study (a / the / Ø) hydrogen and other elements from *(a / the / Ø)* periodic table.
7. The city's new plan to improve public transportation has many potential (*problem / problems*), such as making public transportation both affordable and environmentally friendly.
8. The most important characteristic of (*a / the / Ø*) diamond is (*a / the / Ø*) cut because it determines how much (*a / the / Ø*) diamond will sparkle.

Common Error 1.3 Is the noun plural or not?

furniture is
Amish ~~furnitures are~~ usually 100 percent wood regardless of the style.

REMEMBER: Do not make a non-count noun plural. When it is the subject, use the third person singular verb form.

Common Error 1.4 Does the noun need an article or not?

furniture
People from the Neolithic period (10,2000–2,000 BCE) made ~~a furniture~~ from stone.

REMEMBER: Do not use *a* or *an* with a non-count noun.

ACTIVITY 5 Common Errors 1.3 and 1.4

In each set of sentences, cross out any nouns that are not used correctly. Write the correct nouns and correct any errors in verb forms.

1. Sunlights are a part of the radiation from the sun. When the light is blocked by clouds, the day is not as clear.
2. A blood is made of blood cells. The blood cells are in the blood plasmas, which is made mostly of water.
3. San Francisco is a city that suffers from a great deal of traffics. Traffics includes cars, trucks, and other vehicles. It is important to note that it also includes bicycles, streetcars, and other types of public transportations.
4. Salts is a common mineral found in salt mines. Another common place to find salts is in seawater. The ocean, for example, is over three percent salts.
5. Electrical engineerings is a specific type of engineerings that involves electricity and electronics. Inventions such as semiconductors, graphene, and circuits are items an electrical engineer might study.
6. A good paper requires writers to conduct a research. Writers need to collect informations in order to support their opinions and ideas. Their conclusions will be much more persuasive if the writer includes notes from secondary sources such as newspapers, journals, and reliable Web sites.

Common Error 1.5 Do you need *much* or *a great deal of*?

Brazil produces ~~much~~ *a great deal of* coffee.

REMEMBER: It is not common to use *much* in affirmative statements. Use *a great deal of* instead. It is more common to use *much* in negative statements and questions. In addition, we do not usually use *a lot of* or *lots of* in academic writing.

ACTIVITY 6 Common Error 1.5

Rewrite the sentences to sound more academic.

1. We say: Lots of oil comes from countries in the Middle East.

   We write: ____

   ____

2. We say: The federal government offers a lot of scholarship money for students who want to attend an English-speaking university.

   We write: ____

   ____

3. We say: There is not a lot of international attention focused on the poverty problems faced by some small island nations.

   We write: ____

   ____

4. We say: Not a lot of time was allowed for the members of the jury to decide the fate of the defendant.

   We write: ____

   ____

5. We say: Economists have spent so much time over the past few years studying consumer habits since more shopping is done online.

   We write: ____

   ____

6. We say: Is there a lot of government money dedicated to helping unemployed people find jobs?

   We write: ____

   ____

Academic Vocabulary

Nouns from the Academic Word List

attitude	colleague	distinction	incidence	procedure
bias	device	enforcement	outcome	publication

Source: Academic Word List (Coxhead 2000)

ACTIVITY 7 Vocabulary in Academic Writing

Use the academic vocabulary words to complete the sentences. Use the plural form if needed.

Subject Area	Example from Academic Writing
Science	**1.** Male giraffes can grow to be 18 feet (5.5 meters) tall and females 14 feet (4.3 meters) tall, thus giving giraffes the ______________________ of being the tallest animal in the world.
Literature	**2.** The ______________________ of Shirley Jackson's short story "The Lottery" in 1948 created a great deal of controversy.
Biology	**3.** A microscope is a common ______________________ used by biologists to see cells and organisms that are not visible to the naked eye.
Mathematics	**4.** It is important that students who want a career that requires a great deal of computation are able to accurately use most mathematical ______________________ .
History	**5.** One ______________________ of male suffrage spreading to many countries was women increasing their efforts to obtain the right to vote.
Legal Issues	**6.** Although it may be illegal to download movies from the Internet, ______________________ of the laws is almost impossible due to complications in tracing IP addresses.
Polticial Science	**7.** A recent study determined that there is a link between political ______________________ and age with older voters tending to be more conservative and younger voters leaning toward liberalism.
Health	**8.** Poor eating habits have led to an increased ______________________ of obesity-related diseases, such as diabetes and heart disease.
Business	**9.** With the growing number of online programs, the ______________________ against potential employees who earned their degree online is fading.
Sociology	**10.** One thing that favorably affects someone's opinion about their workplace is how sociable their ______________________ are.

Put It Together

ACTIVITY 8 Review Quiz

Multiple Choice Choose the letter of the correct answer.

1. In ______ cases, temperature plays a role in controlling the amount of pollution in the air.

   a. many **b.** much **c.** a **d.** the

2. A great deal of ______ has been conducted to examine the root causes of tooth decay.

   a. projects **b.** project **c.** researches **d.** research

3. One of ______ top exports for the United States is oil.

   a. an **b.** Ø **c.** a **d.** the

4. Without a doubt, the number of visitors to the Colosseum in Rome contributes to ______ tourism dollars for Italy.

   a. much **b.** lots of **c.** a **d.** a large number of

5. Despite many developments being made with self-driving cars, there are still several ______ that require solutions, such as better and more detailed maps so the cars will know exactly where to go.

   a. an problem **b.** the problems **c.** problems **d.** problem

Error Correction One of the five underlined words or phrases is not correct. Find the error and correct it. Be prepared to explain your answer.

6. Many environmental organizations believe hybrid cars will help reduce carbon emissions. However, it will take a large number of time before car manufacturers are able to stop producing cars that use gasoline and focus their attention on making more hybrid vehicles.

7. The government should invest more of its budget in science and math education to inspire a large number of students to pursue a careers in engineering.

8. A great risk in working with a great deal of mosquitoes to study malaria involves the chance of being bitten and contracting a disease from the bite.

On a day with high levels of pollution, a man wears a mask in front of the Forbidden City in Beijing, China.

ACTIVITY 9 Building Greater Sentences

Combine these short sentences into one sentence. You can add new words and move words around, but you should not add or omit any ideas. More than one answer is possible, but all of these sentences require noun phrases. (See Appendix 1, Building Greater Sentences, page 224, for tips on how to do this activity.)

1. **a.** Environmentalists are thinking about China's pollution problem.
   b. The problem needs to be solved.
   c. A lot of rules will hurt the country's industries.

   ____

   ____

2. **a.** Mechanical engineering is important.
   b. It is important in modern society.
   c. One reason for its importance is that it develops machines.
   d. Those machines can help save a great number of lives.
   e. Those machines are important.

   ____

   ____

3. **a.** Mexico and Guatemala are different.
   b. Mexico produces a lot of oil.
   c. Guatemala does not produce a lot of oil.
   d. The two countries are neighbors.

   ____

   ____

ACTIVITY 10 Steps to Composing

Read the paragraph. Then follow the directions in the 10 steps below to edit the information and composition of the paragraph. Write your revised paragraph on a separate sheet of paper. Be careful with capitalization and punctuation. Check your answers with the class.

PROBLEM–SOLUTION PARAGRAPH

Job Satisfaction of Hospital Doctors

[1] A recent survey that was published in a scientific journal showed that the average doctor is not happy with the hospital he or she works in. [2] One reason for this situation is the fact that there are not enough doctors to care for all the patients in the hospital. [3] They are working so many hours and are not giving the best service because they are too tired. [4] They claim they were not aware of the time they were going to have to work or how difficult it would be. [5] The easiest way to solve this problem is for hospitals to have more doctors or allow doctors more time off. [6] However, this problem needs to be addressed before doctors begin work. [7] Medical schools need to better prepare students for the workload and the time constraints of being a hospital doctor. [8] Medical students need to know that they will need to dedicate a lot of time if they continue into professional medicine.

1. In sentence 1, change *the average* to *many* and make necessary changes so that the other nouns and verbs in the sentence agree.
2. In advanced academic writing, combine sentences that have a logical connection. Combine sentences 2 and 3 using the conjunction *so*.
3. The word *so* is very common in spoken English. In sentence 3, change the phrase *so many* to *a large number of* before the noun *hours*.
4. In academic writing, try to be specific when possible. Change the noun *time* to the noun phrase *many hours* in sentence 4.

5. In sentence 4, add *that there would be a great deal of difficulty* in place of *how difficult it would be* in order to have two parallel structures.

6. The verb *have* in sentence 5 is a weak verb. Change *have* to another verb with a more concrete meaning.

7. To use more specific language, change sentence 5 to include the phrase *a great deal of.*

8. Make *doctors* singular in sentence 6 and change the article and verb appropriately.

9. In sentence 7, be more specific by adding the word *many* before the noun phrase *time constraints.*

10. In sentence 8, change one example of spoken language to appropriate academic language.

ACTIVITY 11 Original Writing

On a separate sheet of paper, write a problem–solution paragraph (at least seven sentences). Use several noun phrases and underline them.

Here are some examples of how to begin.

- *Fast food can cause many problems. One problem . . .*
- *Many students do not want to take a lot of math and science courses. One reason for this might be because . . .*
- *College students face a large number of challenges during their first semester . . .*

Visitors in the Centro de Arte Reina Sofia in Madrid, Spain, view Pablo Picasso's *Guernica.*

Writing about the Past

WHAT DO YOU KNOW?

DISCUSS Look at the photo and read the caption. Discuss the questions.

1. Pablo Picasso is famous for his use of color. Why do you think he painted this work in shades of black and gray?
2. When did you last visit a museum? What painting or exhibit made an impression on you?

FIND THE ERRORS This paragraph contains two errors with past verb forms. Find the errors and correct them. Explain your corrections to a partner.

DESCRIPTIVE PARAGRAPH

Guernica

[1] Pablo Picasso's painting *Guernica* is one of the most powerful antiwar statements of all time. [2] The artist was painting it in response to the German bombing of the Basque town of Guernica, Spain, in April 1937. [3] The painting is actually an enormous mural, about 25 feet wide and 11 feet tall, painted in stark shades of black, white, and gray. [4] Some of the striking images include a bull standing over a woman with a dead child in her arms; a wounded, terrified horse; and a dead soldier holding a broken sword with a flower growing out of it. [5] Other symbols of hope, in contrast to the devastation or war, include a lamp and a dove. [6] Picasso completed the painting in June 1937 while he had lived in Paris. [7] Today the painting hangs in the Museo Reina Sofia in Madrid.

Grammar Forms

2.1 Simple Past

Subject	Verb	Example
I / he / she / it / you / we / they	verb + *-ed* (regular)	Picasso **painted** *Guernica* in April 1937 in response to the German bombing of Guernica, Spain.
	went (irregular)	In 1982, Britain **went** to war with Argentina over the Falkland Islands.
	did not + verb (regular and irregular verb)	The United States **did not enter** World War II until after the Japanese attack on Pearl Harbor.

Note
See Appendix 4, Irregular Verbs, for irregular verb forms.

2.2 Past Progressive

Subject	Verb	Example
I / he / she / it	*was* (*not*) + verb + *-ing*	By the beginning of 2011, the economy **was beginning** to recover from the recession of 2008. The economic forecast **was not looking** as bleak.
you / we / they	*were* (*not*) + verb + *-ing*	The artifacts suggested that at least two different groups of people **were living** in the area in the 5th century. Researchers **were not looking** for the artifacts when they found them.

2.3 Past Perfect

Subject	Verb	Example
I / he / she / it / you / we / they	*had* (*not*) + past participle of verb	By the time the company removed the hacker's message from the Web site, it **had gone** viral.

Note
See Appendix 4, Irregular Verbs, for irregular verb forms.

ACTIVITY 1

Fill in the blank with the indicated past form of the verb in parentheses.

1. Picasso ______________________________ (*live*) in Paris when he painted his masterpiece, *Guernica*. (past progressive)

2. Jones and Markham's important 1999 research study ______________________________ (*focus*) on what teachers ______________________________ (*do*) in bilingual classrooms in Canada. (simple past; past progressive)

3. When he ______________________________ (*be*) 32 years old, Bill Gates ______________________________ (*already, make*) a billion dollars, and was one of the wealthiest people in the world. (simple past; past perfect)

4. Some people in the study stopped breathing while they ______________________________ (*sleep*) because they had a condition called sleep apnea. (past progressive)

5. Legendary rock star David Bowie ______________________________ (*know*) about his terminal liver cancer for over a year before his death in January of 2016. After his death, close friends revealed that the star ______________________________ (*want*) desperately to remain alive. (past perfect; past perfect)

6. On November 22, 1963, U.S. president John F. Kennedy was assassinated while he and his wife ______________________________ (*ride*) in an open car in Dallas, Texas. (past progressive)

7. Over 75 percent of dog bites to the face occurred while the person ______________________________ (*bend*) over the dog. (past progressive)

8. In 1803, novelist Jane Austen ______________________________ (*live*) in the English city of Bath when she started *The Watsons*, a new novel that she never ______________________________ (*complete*). (past progressive; simple past)

Common Uses

2.4 Using Simple Past

The simple past is commonly used in writing to describe an action completed in the past. It is used:

1. to report historical or past events	The war **ended** in 1945.
2. to explain how an event occurred in a process analysis	When the rains finally **arrived**, the crops **grew** quickly, and the water reservoirs **began** to fill.
3. to describe methods or results of experiments in reports	After the nurse **administered** the medication, the patient's heart rate **returned** to normal.
4. to describe case studies or research findings	In the 2015 study, researchers **found** evidence of improvement in student math scores.
5. to describe events in narrative essays	Elon Musk **had** a difficult childhood, but as an adult, he **graduated** from an Ivy League college and **started** several successful companies.

2.5 Using Past Progressive

The past progressive is not very common in academic writing. It is mainly used to write about:

1. an action that was in progress at or around a specific time in the past • Often used when setting the scene or background of a narrative • Common time expressions include: *at the time, at that moment, by (2010), in (1986)* • Common adverbs: *already, still*	SLEEPING TORNADO HIT — NOW At the moment the tornado hit, most inhabitants **were sleeping**. At 10:00 p.m., the sun **was** just **setting** in the far-north town of Barrow, Alaska. About 30 percent of the young adults surveyed **were** still **living** at home.
2. an action that was in progress when another (shorter) event occurred. Frequently, the shorter action interrupts the longer one. • Often used in reports of what happened • Common to use *when / while / as* + past progressive for the action in progress • Common to use *before / until / when* + simple past for the shorter action	On December 8, 1980, Mark David Chapman shot former Beatle John Lennon as the singer **was entering** his apartment building.

2.5 Using Past Progressive (Continued)

3. to write about two or more actions that were in progress at the same time in the past	
• Used for actions of a longer duration in any kind of report of what happened	While the children **were participating** in the mapmaking activity, the researchers **were observing** them through a one-way mirror.
• Often, the simple past is used instead of the progressive in one of the clauses	While the children **were participating** in the mapmaking activity, the researchers **observed** them through a one-way mirror.

2.6 Using Past Perfect

The past perfect is not very common in writing. It is used for:

	XXX (RATIFIED) — X (1945) — I (NOW)
1. the first or older of two or more completed actions in the past	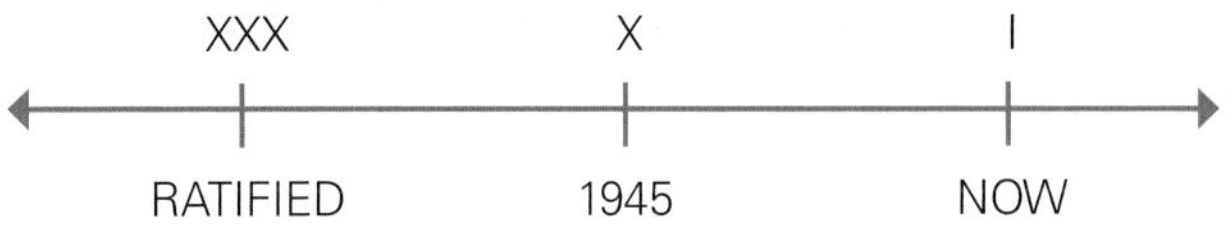 The United Nations officially **began** in October of 1945 when most of the original participating countries **had ratified** its charter.
2. the condition in a past hypothetical sentence	The United States did not enter World War II until 1941. If it **had entered** earlier, the war may have ended earlier.
3. background information that explains a sequence of events	The patient entered the hospital at 10:00 p.m. with stomach pains. She **had eaten** shellfish.
4. the earlier of two completed actions when the first begins with a time clause with *by* or *by the time*	The company **had** already **launched** a new prototype by the time its rival **released** its latest creation.

Note
Often, when the time frame is clear, the simple past is used instead of the past perfect for the earlier event. When adverb clauses include *before* or *after*, for example, the simple past is just as clear.

Before Germany bombed Spain, Picasso was not very interested in painting about the war.

Before Germany bombed Spain, Picasso had not been very interested in painting about the war.

ACTIVITY 2

For each sentence, fill in the blank with a correct past form of the verb in parentheses. For some sentences, more than one answer may be possible.

1. The worst wildfire in California history occurred in the San Diego area in 2003. One year after the devastating fire, however, biologists found encouraging signs that the burned area ______________________ (*begin*) to recover.

2. Diana, Princess of Wales, died in a car crash on August 31, 1997. At the time, she ______________________ (*not wear*) a seatbelt.

3. According to the case study notes, the patient ______________________ (*experience*) shortness of breath for several months before she finally made an appointment to see a doctor.

4. Automation was relatively late to enter the Japanese banking system. For example, in the 1970s, when most American banks ______________________ (*already use*) computers, banks in Japan ______________________ (*still use*) the abacus to make calculations.

5. In the tsunami that hit Indonesia and Thailand in 2004, the death toll was very high because people ______________________ (*go*) about their daily lives, unaware of the imminent danger.

6. Taxicabs in New York City must have a license, called a medallion. In 2013, the medallions ______________________ (*cost*) as much as $1.3 million each.

7. The purpose of this research project was to study eye movements of young readers as they encountered easy and difficult material in a passage. As a child ______________________ (*read*), a computer program ______________________ (*record*) her eye movements.

8. A 2015 study indicated that, due to the high price of printed textbooks, e-book use among college students ______________________ (*increase*) rapidly in just a few years.

Common Errors

Common Error 2.1 Do you need simple past or simple present?

The report showed that climate change ~~was~~ is a huge problem.

REMEMBER: Use simple present when talking about facts or situations that exist in the present, not only the past.

ACTIVITY 3 Common Error 2.1

For each sentence, fill in each blank with the simple past or simple present form of the verb in parentheses.

1. More than 50 years after President Kennedy ______________ (*sign*) the Equal Pay Act, the gap between salaries for men and women ______________ (*remain*) a problem today.

2. Last year's study ______________ (*find*) that in the last decade the pay gap ______________ (*become*) greater the longer a person was in the workforce.

3. The United States is one of few countries in the developed world that currently ______________ (*use*) the death penalty. Mexico, its neighbor to the south, ______________ (*end*) the death penalty in 2005.

4. During the 1950s and 1960s, Martin Luther King, Jr., ______________ (*lead*) the civil rights movement in the United States. Civil rights ______________ (*include*) the right to vote, the right to a fair trial, and the right to an education.

5. Fifteen nations ______________ (*make up*) the UN Security Council. The Security Council ______________ (*hold*) its first session on January 17, 1946, in London.

Common Error 2.2 Do you need verb + *-ing*?

The flight was ~~go~~ *going* smoothly when the pilot suddenly received a radio report about an approaching storm.

REMEMBER: Add *-ing* to the main verb in the past progressive.

ACTIVITY 4 Common Error 2.2

Read each sentence. If the verb form is correct, write *C* on the line. If it is wrong, write *X* on the line. Then underline the error and write the correction above it.

______ **1.** In 1988, Barack Obama was work as a community activist when he was accepted to Harvard Law School.

______ **2.** The refugee camp was a busy place. More aid workers were arriving from the capital city, and others were unloading the trucks and distributing food.

______ **3.** Countrywide Financial Corporation was the first bank to fail in the 2008 mortgage lending crisis. As everyone was wonder what might happen next, other large investment firms soon followed.

______ **4.** The presidential candidates were argue when the news commentator asked them a question about health care.

______ **5.** After an earthquake, many people say they will never forget what they were do when the earth started shaking.

______ **6.** According to the U.S. Census Bureau, approximately 63 percent of Americans were live in cities in 2013.

Common Error 2.3 Do you need simple past or past progressive?

were watching
The prisoner escaped while the guards ~~watched~~ a soccer game.

REMEMBER: Use past progressive to emphasize an action that was in progress. The simple past is used for an interrupting action or an action of much shorter duration.

ACTIVITY 5 Common Error 2.3

For each group of sentences, fill in each blank with the simple past or past progressive form of the verb in parentheses.

1. Throughout April of 1975, the North Vietnamese army ______________________ (*move*) closer and closer to Saigon while the South Vietnamese opposition ______________________ (*collapse*). Finally, on April 30, the North Vietnamese army ______________________ (*enter*) Saigon, and the South Vietnamese president ______________________ (*surrender*).

2. The Detroit Lions football team ______________________ (*host*) the Chicago Bears at Tiger Stadium on October 24, 1971. Late in the game, player Chuck Hughes ______________________ (*run*) with the ball when suddenly he ______________________ (*fall*) to the ground and ______________________ (*die*). Later, doctors ______________________ (*discover*) that Hughes ______________________ (*suffer*) from heart disease and that one of his arteries was 75 percent blocked. He was only 28 years old.

3. The 1980s saw the height of the low-fat food movement in the United States. By the 1990s, Americans ______________________ (*eat*) less fat, but they ______________________ (*not become*) any thinner.

4. The Post-it Note was invented by accident. In 1968, an engineer named Spencer Silver ______________________ (*work*) for the 3M company. He ______________________ (*try*) to develop a super-strong glue for use in the aerospace industry. Instead, he ______________________ (*invent*) a glue that could be peeled off and reused. Spencer ______________________ (*call*) his invention "a solution without a problem" because at the time, no one could imagine any use for it.

Sticky notes cover the message board at the Times Square Information Center in New York City.

Common Error 2.4 Do you need simple past or past perfect?

The Wright brothers ~~had invented~~ invented the first successful flying machine in 1903. People had tried to fly in self-powered planes before the Wright brothers ~~had been~~ were successful.

REMEMBER: Use past perfect only when you need to make clear which of two or more past actions happened first. Use past perfect for the earlier event(s). If there is only one event, use simple past.

ACTIVITY 6 Common Error 2.4

For each set of sentences, fill in each blank with the simple past or past perfect form of the verb in parentheses. Think about which event happened first.

1. By the time John Wilkes Booth ______________________ (*shoot*) Abraham Lincoln, the Civil War ______________________ (*end*) with General Lee's surrender five days earlier.

2. Nelson Mandela ______________________ (*spend*) 26 years in prison when he ______________________ (*walk*) out in 1990.

3. On March 11, 2011, a terrible earthquake ______________________ (*hit*) Japan. Few scientists ______________________ (*predict*) such a strong earthquake and its resulting tsunami, so the country ______________________ (*be*) unprepared on that day. The tsunami ______________________ (*damage*) a nuclear reactor. About 230,000 people ______________________ (*lose*) their homes.

4. By the early part of the 20th century, many African-Americans ______________________ (*move*) from the rural south to northern cities. In the South, they ______________________ (*make*) their living primarily on farms until insects ______________________ (*cause*) severe crop damage. They ______________________ (*go*) to cities like Chicago to find jobs.

5. At the beginning of the Harry Potter series of books by J. K. Rowling, the hero, Harry Potter, ______________________ (*live*) with his aunt and uncle. His parents ______________________ (*die*) when he ______________________ (*be*) a baby. Fortunately, a letter ______________________ (*arrive*) one day informing him of his acceptance to Hogwarts, which ______________________ (*change*) his future forever.

Academic Vocabulary

Verbs Frequently Used in Past Progressive in Academic English

become	get	look	take	use
do	have	make	try	work

Source: Corpus of Contemporary American English (Davies 2008–)

ACTIVITY 7 Vocabulary in Academic Writing

Use the academic vocabulary words in the past progressive to complete the sentences.

Subject Area	Example from Academic Writing
Education	**1.** The World Bank estimated in 2012 that 31 million school-age girls did not receive an adequate education and suggested that countries ________________ (not) enough steps to improve their education.
Psychology	**2.** Many participants in the study reported that they slept well while they ________________ but experienced more sleep disruption after they retired.
Medicine	**3.** One and a half years after her operation, the patient ________________ well, with no tumor regrowth and no other reported complications.
Environmental Studies	**4.** By the end of the year 2000, about 1 million homes worldwide ________________ their electricity from solar cells, and about 700,000 of these were in villages in developing countries.
Urban Planning	**5.** As wealthy developers began buying up older properties and developing them, it ________________ more difficult for lower-income workers to find affordable housing on the West side.
History	**6.** In 1963, female workers in the United States ________________ 59 cents for every dollar that a man earned.
Music Education	**7.** After asking the child to sing any song he knew, the teacher realized that he ________________ trouble singing a tune.
Archaeology	**8.** By 500,000 years ago, early humans ________________ long wooden spears to kill large animals.
Marketing	**9.** While conducting market research prior to developing the next generation of smartphones, researchers learned that users ________________ for smaller phones with features like games and cameras.
Asian Studies	**10.** The 1970s and 1980s were a time when many Asian nations ________________ to modernize and at the same time preserve their ancient traditions and values.

Put It Together

ACTIVITY 8 Review Quiz

Multiple Choice Choose the letter of the correct answer.

1. While the lions in the wild animal park ______, the tourists took photos from a safe distance.

   a. ate **b.** were eating **c.** Both answers are possible.

2. The candidates ______ polite to each other during the debate even though they had criticized each other strongly in interviews leading up to it.

   a. were **b.** had been **c.** Both answers are possible.

3. Even after word processing became popular, many famous authors ______ their manuscripts by hand or on a typewriter.

   a. still wrote **b.** were still writing **c.** Both answers are possible.

4. By 2014, over 110,000 Saudi students ______ in the United States, and the number continued to grow.

   a. studied **b.** were studying **c.** Both answers are possible.

5. Before the first Europeans arrived, native people ______ in North America for thousands of years.

   a. lived **b.** had lived **c.** Both answers are possible.

Error Correction One of the five underlined words or phrases is not correct. Find the error and correct it. Be prepared to explain your answer.

6. Although Antarctica has no permanent residents, approximately 4,000 people was living there in 2015. The residents included citizens of 29 different countries. Most of them were scientists who were doing research in the area.

7. At 8:30 a.m., a Los Angeles Zoo employee was working near the gorilla habitat when he slipped and fell into the enclosure. Firefighters were called to rescue the man. The gorillas hardly noticed the incident because they slept in another location.

8. Desktop computers may become obsolete as more and more people use mobile devices such as tablets or smartphones to access the Internet. According to a recent report, a surprising 11.3 percent of Americans using mobile devices exclusively to access the Internet in 2015, which is up from 10.6 percent in 2014.

New Yorkers enjoy a sunny spring day in Union Square.

ACTIVITY 9 Building Greater Sentences

Combine these short sentences about the past into one sentence. You can add new words and move words around, but you should not add or omit any ideas. More than one answer is possible.

1. **a.** Jennifer Lawrence is the star of *The Hunger Games*.
   b. She was discovered at age 14.
   c. She was walking through Union Square in New York.
   d. She was walking with her mother.

   ____

   ____

2. **a.** The Internet became a popular tool for research.
   b. Before that, people were using print encyclopedias such as the *Encyclopedia Britannica.*
   c. The people needed information.
   d. They used them for hundreds of years.

   ____

   ____

3. **a.** Roy J. Glauber was sleeping.
   b. The time was 5:36 a.m.
   c. He received the news.
   d. The news was that he had won a prize.
   e. The prize was the 2005 Nobel Prize.
   f. The Nobel Prize was for physics.

   ____

   ____

ACTIVITY 10 **Steps to Composing**

Read the paragraph. Then follow the directions in the 10 steps to edit the information and composition of the paragraph. Write your revised paragraph on a separate sheet of paper. Be careful with capitalization and punctuation. Check your answers with the class.

NARRATIVE PARAGRAPH

The 1989 World Series

[1] October 17 was the day of the third game of the 1989 World Series baseball championship. [2] The game was in San Francisco. [3] Sixty-two thousand people were attending the game at Candlestick Park. [4] The game was just starting at 5:04 p.m. [5] Suddenly a powerful earthquake struck. [6] The magnitude 6.9 earthquake caused approximately $6 billion in damage in the San Francisco Bay area. [7] It caused 63 deaths and almost 4,000 injuries. [8] But the destruction was not as great as it might have been because of an unusual coincidence. [9] Both of the teams that were playing in the World Series—the San Francisco Giants and the Oakland Athletics—were from the bay area. [10] Because of this, many people had left work early to attend the game or watch it at home with their families. [11] Many others had stayed in the city after work. [12] They watched the game with colleagues. [13] Traffic was lighter than usual. [14] No doubt this prevented many deaths. [15] The earthquake was memorable for another reason as well. [16] Because of the television coverage of the baseball game, it became the first major earthquake that was seen live by people all over the country.

1. In sentence 2, delete *The game was*, then combine sentences 1 and 2.
2. Replace *Suddenly* with *when* in sentence 5 and combine sentences 4 and 5.
3. To avoid repetition of the same word, replace *earthquake* with the synonyms *quake* or *temblor* in sentence 6 and one other place.
4. Replace *caused* with *was responsible for* in sentence 7.
5. Do not start a sentence with a conjunction in academic writing. Replace *But* with *However* and a comma in sentence 8.
6. Use the past progressive to emphasize an action in progress. Replace *watched* with *were watching* in sentence 12.

7. Combine sentences 11 and 12.

8. Begin sentence 13 with *Consequently* or a similar transition word or phrase.

9. In sentence 16, use a synonym for *Because of*.

10. Replace *people* with *baseball lovers* in sentence 16.

ACTIVITY 11 Original Writing

On a separate sheet of paper, write a narrative paragraph (at least seven sentences) about an historical event that interests you. Use at least one example of the past progressive to establish the background of the narrative and underline it; try to use at least two if possible.

Here are some examples of how to begin.

- *It was April 14, 1912, the fifth night of the first voyage of the luxury ship* Titanic. *At around 11:30 p.m., most of the ship's passengers were already sleeping in their rooms.*
- *The year was 1876. Two men, Alexander Graham Bell and Elisha Gray, were racing against the clock to be the first to file a patent for a device that could transmit speech electrically—the telephone.*

Twelve-year-old students use their own electronic devices as they work together in a class in New Smyrna Beach, Florida.

3 Using the Present Perfect

WHAT DO YOU KNOW?

DISCUSS Look at the photo and read the caption. Discuss the questions.

1. How do you think working together can help these students?
2. Have you recently worked in a small group in class? Do you think it is a good strategy? Why or why not?

FIND THE ERRORS This paragraph contains two errors with the present perfect. Find the errors and correct them. Explain your corrections to a partner.

DESCRIPTIVE PARAGRAPH

Flipped Classrooms

[1] In recent years, some schools and colleges begin to experiment with a different approach to classroom content. [2] In the past, students listened to lectures in class, and then they did additional activities at home. [3] They applied what they had learned in school as they completed exercises, solved problems, or wrote essays. [4] In the 1990s, some educators have proposed a new strategy—flipping the classroom. [5] In a flipped classroom approach, students learn through a variety of methods, including small group discussions with peers. [6] Students watch lectures online at home or anywhere they have computer access, and then they do activities in class, often in groups, under the guidance of the teacher.

Grammar Forms

3.1 Present Perfect

Subject	Verb	Example
I / you / we / they	*have* (*not*) + past participle	Advances in technology **have not expanded** economic opportunities for everyone.
he / she / it	*has* (*not*) + past participle	The drop in oil prices **has caused** turmoil in the stock market.

Notes

1. The past participle of regular verbs is the same as the simple past form: verb + *-ed (expanded, caused).*
2. The past participle of irregular verbs varies (*had, been, brought*). See Appendix 4, Irregular Verbs, for a list of irregular verbs.

ACTIVITY 1

Read each sentence. Fill in the blank with the correct present perfect form of the verb in parentheses.

1. Since the oil leak, a chemical oceanographer ________________ (*study*) the composition of the seawater near the oil accident. The results are discouraging.
2. In the last 200 years, the population of the planet ________________ (*increase*) from 1 billion to over 7 billion people, and scientists estimate that it will continue to grow.
3. The evidence indicates that a new species of bird ________________ (*begin*) migrating to the area.
4. Scientists ________________ (*find*) a planet of a similar size to Earth and a similar distance from a star or sun.
5. The number of shared offices, or coworking spaces, ________________ (*grow*) in recent years.
6. Since 1999, deaths from prescription opioid drug overdose ________________ (*rise*) 400 percent in the United States.
7. ________________ (*you / consider*) going on an adventure abroad? According to many international travel Web sites, more people than ever will travel to another country in the next year.
8. Despite pressures from the outside world, some indigenous peoples ________________ (*not / join*) mainstream society yet.

Common Uses

3.2 Using Present Perfect

The present perfect is important in academic writing because it performs several different functions. It is used to talk about:

1. an action that began in the past and is still true or continues until now • Common with *since* + point in time or *for* + length of time	PAST 1955 NOW FUTURE An effective vaccine against polio **has existed** since 1955 / for over 60 years.
2. a past accomplishment or change that is important in the present (no specific time) • Common adverbs are *recently* and *not ... yet.*	Economists **have** recently **recommended** raising the minimum wage. Scientists **have not eradicated** malaria yet. Scientists **have not** yet **eradicated** malaria.
3. a past action that has happened multiple times (no specific time) and may happen again • Common adverbs are *many, several,* and *(number) times.*	PAST NOW FUTURE A human **has walked** on the moon at least 12 times.
4. an action or thought experienced (or not) at any time in the past (no specific time) • An opening question is possible in a paragraph or essay. • Common adverbs are *ever* and *never.*	**Have** you ever **wondered** how ice cream is made? The astronaut **has** never **completed** a space walk.

3.3 Using Present Perfect in Paragraphs

The present perfect is often confused with other verb forms, especially the simple past. It is helpful to recognize common patterns and uses in paragraphs. Present perfect is often used:

1. to introduce a paragraph or new topic about a present routine or habitual activity • The present perfect describes an event relevant to the present topic, and then other present forms are used to give more detail.	Seals **have made** a big comeback on northeast Atlantic beaches, but the seals **have brought** another species with them: the great whites. Great white sharks **are** vital for our ecosystem, and researchers **are** glad to see they **are** alive and well. Beachgoers, however, **are** not as happy.
2. to introduce a narrative about a past event • The present perfect gives information to set up the past event; then other past forms are used to elaborate on the event.	U.S. politician Gary Johnson **has climbed** the "Seven Summits," or the seven highest mountains on the seven continents. On May 30, 2003, he **reached** the peak of Mount Everest even though suffering from frostbite.

Source: *The grammar book: Form, meaning, and use for English language teachers* (Larsen-Freeman & Celce-Murcia 2016)

ACTIVITY 2

Fill in the blank with the correct present perfect, simple present, or simple past form of the verb in parentheses.

1. Climate change ________________ (*affect*) polar bears for a number of years.
2. Since 1965, nearly 59 million immigrants ________________ (*arrive*) in the United States. In the 1970s, many of the new Americans ________________ (*arrive*) as refugees from wars in Southeast Asia.
3. The Chinese ________________ (*be*) at the forefront of innovation for thousands of years. During the ninth century, they ________________ (*invent*) gunpowder.
4. ________________ (*you / ever / wonder*) how birds learn to sing their particular songs? Most species of birds ________________ (*learn*) to sing during a critical period in their development.
5. In many countries around the world, women ________________ (*make*) a lot of progress in the last 100 years. They ________________ (*fight for and win*) the right to vote in 1920.
6. According to researchers, in all likelihood, humans ________________ (*already, reach*) their maximum life span. The oldest humans today ________________ (*live*) about 115 years.
7. Since 2008, electric cars ________________ (*become*) increasingly popular. However, William Morrison ________________ (*produce*) the first electric car in the United States in 1890.

Common Errors

Common Error 3.1 Do you need present perfect or simple present?

have become
In recent years, many teachers ~~become~~ dissatisfied with their profession because of the increasing emphasis on testing.

REMEMBER: If the action or experience began in the past and is still true, use present perfect. Look for words such as *recent, recently, lately, for / since.* Use simple present when talking about general facts.

ACTIVITY 3 **Common Error 3.1**

For each set of sentences, underline the correct form of the words in parentheses.

1. Since 2015, South America (*experiences / has experienced*) an increase in infection by the Zika virus. Mosquitoes (*carry / have carried*) the virus and spread it to humans. People are concerned because this virus (*causes / has caused*) birth defects.

2. Elephants typically (*have / have had*) a complex social structure led by matriarchs, or older females. Unfortunately, in recent years older elephants (*are / have been*) the target of poachers who want the ivory in their tusks. As a result, younger females (*begin / have begun*) to lead groups that (*lose / have lost*) their matriarchs.

3. Wolves, caribou, and moose all (*live / have lived*) in Denali Park in Alaska; wolves (*are / have been*) the predators, and caribou and moose (*are / have been*) their prey. To help caribou and moose populations grow, the state (*increases / has increased*) its wolf reduction program in some areas recently. This may be one reason why the number of wolves in Denali Park (*drops / has dropped*) in the last 10 years.

4. Last week's report marked the first time that doctors (*recommend / have recommended*) that pregnant women get a mental health check. Research shows that pregnant women often (*experience / have experienced*) some degree of depression.

5. For decades, match fixing (*is / has been*) an ongoing concern in many sports. In recent years, two popular sports, tennis and soccer, (*have / have had*) reports of players intentionally losing games.

6. Most employees (*spend / have spent*) about one-third of their day at work. In a recent study, researchers (*show / have shown*) that good relationships with coworkers (*make / has made*) us healthier.

Common Error 3.2 Do you need present perfect or simple past?

A 2008 study ~~has found~~ found that regular practice of tai chi reduces blood pressure.

Access to the Internet ~~became~~ has become more important than ever.

REMEMBER:
- Use simple past with specific past times such as *yesterday, last* (*month*), (*one year*) *ago,* and *in 2001*. Do not use present perfect with these specific past time words.
- When no specific past time is given, use present perfect for an important change or accomplishment that is relevant in the present.

ACTIVITY 4 Common Error 3.2

Fill in the blank with the simple past or present perfect form of the verb in parentheses.

1. In 2008, the housing market ________________ (*collapse*) as a result of bad lending practices.
2. More than 100 years ago, Henry Morton Stanley ________________ (*explore*) Africa in search of the missionary Dr. David Livingstone.
3. Researchers ________________ (*study*) the Hadza, a group of hunter-gatherers in Africa, in hopes of learning learn more about sleeping patterns.
4. Humans ________________ (*change*) the composition of the atmosphere through their activities.
5. Because of their constant use of digital devices, students ________________ (*lose*) the ability to concentrate when reading long texts online.
6. The availability of junk food in schools, especially soda, as well as a reduction in recess time ________________ (*lead*) to a very worrisome increase in childhood obesity.
7. During the first half of the 20th century, inventions and other innovations ________________ (*improve*) the quality of life in developed countries.
8. The first personal computers ________________ (*come*) on the market in the 1970s, often as kits.
9. Britain ________________ (*vote*) to leave the European Union in 2016.
10. The Internet ________________ (*make*) personal privacy more difficult to maintain.

Academic Vocabulary

Verbs Frequently Used in Present Perfect in Academic Writing

be	come	have	make	show
become	find	lead	see	take

Source: Corpus of Contemporary American English (Davies 2008–)

ACTIVITY 5 Vocabulary in Academic Writing

Use the academic vocabulary words in the present perfect to complete the sentences.

Subject Area	Example from Academic Writing
Education	**1.** Students in the immersion program ________________ more progress in learning a second language than other students have.
Political Science	**2.** Many of the protestors at the candidate's recent speeches ________________ to the United States as immigrants.
Environmental Science	**3.** Recently, scientists ________________ increasingly alarmed about the destruction of coral reefs.
Social Studies	**4.** The increase in heroin availability ________________ to the recent increases in substance abuse, crime, and death by overdose.
Psychology	**5.** Researchers ________________ brain scans, which are like a kind of photo or imaging, that show the brains of serial killers have certain characteristics.
Health	**6.** Patients who were given the medication ________________ signs of improvement already.
Economics	**7.** According to economists, raising the minimum wage ________________ some effect on poverty.
Anthropology	**8.** Researchers ________________ evidence of violent death in human skeletons near a lake in Africa, indicating that humans may have engaged in warfare 10,000 years ago.
Biology	**9.** By treating ants with chemical compounds, scientists ________________ able to change their behavior.
English Composition	**10.** From what I ________________ of American society so far, I believe I have made a decision that will change my life.

Put It Together

ACTIVITY 6 Review Quiz

Multiple Choice Choose the letter of the correct answer.

1. Astronomers ______ a possible ninth planet in our solar system.

   a. discover **b.** discovered **c.** have discovered **d.** discovers

2. The economy ______ in the last few years, yet there are indicators that it will start to recover in the next year.

   a. worsen **b.** worsened **c.** has worsened **d.** is worsening

3. In recent years, researchers ______ to investigate the link between microorganisms in our gut and our mood.

   a. begin **b.** began **c.** have begun **d.** will begin

4. Prior to Hurricane Katrina, engineers and politicians ______ the best way to keep floodwaters out of New Orleans.

   a. debate **b.** debated **c.** have debated **d.** should debate

5. Studies have shown that eating a plant-based diet ______ healthier than one that includes a lot of animal products.

   a. is **b.** was **c.** has been **d.** will have been

Error Correction One of the five underlined words or phrases is not correct. Find the error and correct it. Be prepared to explain your answer.

6. Since 2010, when the debt crisis first had began in Greece, most private investors have sold their property there, and other countries have taken on Greece's debt.

7. A group of researchers, including anthropologists, human rights groups, and biologists, have recent determined that nearly a million forest people live in central Africa, mostly in areas where they are able to hunt and fish.

8. More than a decade has passed since one of the deadliest tsunamis killed more than 200,000 people in 14 countries, most of them in Indonesia, after an earthquake with a magnitude of 9.1 has shifted the ocean floor.

ACTIVITY 7 Building Greater Sentences

Combine these short sentences into one sentence. You can add new words and move words around, but you should not add or omit any ideas. More than one answer is possible, but all of these sentences require present perfect.

1. a. Changes happen to trees and shrubs.
   b. They happen in the fall.
   c. Scientists work to understand these changes.
   d. Scientists have done this for years.

   ____

   ____

2. a. There has been a steadily growing concern about the admission process.
   b. This process is for admission to a college.
   c. This occurred over recent years.
   d. The concern is about admission at the most respected American colleges.
   e. The concern is about admission at the most selective American colleges.

   ____

   ____

3. a. 2015 was the hottest year in recorded history by far.
   b. Scientists reported this.
   c. This report came on Wednesday.
   d. This broke a record.
   e. The record was set the year before.

   ____

   ____

ACTIVITY 8 Steps to Composing

Read the paragraph. Then follow the directions in the 10 steps to edit the information and composition of the paragraph. Write your revised paragraph on a separate sheet of paper. Be careful with capitalization and punctuation. Check your answers with the class.

NARRATIVE PARAGRAPH

A Brief History of Flight

[1] Throughout the course of history, humans have wanted to fly like birds. [2] In ancient times, the Greeks told the story of Daedalus, who made wings for himself and his son Icarus out of feathers and wax. [3] In the 15th century, Leonardo da Vinci designed a flying machine called the Ornithopter. [4] Although he never actually built his flying machine, the modern-day helicopter is very similar to his design. [5] In the 18th and 19th centuries, people invented hot-air balloons and gliders. [6] There were also many attempts to build a powered airplane. [7] It was not until the beginning of the 20th century that these efforts were successful. [8] Wilbur and Orville Wright built and flew a motorized airplane for the first time for 120 feet (37 meters) in 1903. [9] The airplane has changed our lives dramatically. [10] Once it took months or even years to cross the ocean, but now travelers make the trip in hours. [11] Because of airplanes, we are able to see other countries, eat new food, and learn about other cultures firsthand.

1. In sentence 1, replace *fly* with *soar above the earth* to avoid overuse of words related to *fly.*

2. In sentence 2, replace *in ancient times* with *thousands of years ago.*

3. It is not good to repeat the same word in adjoining sentences. In sentence 4, replace *flying machine* with *invention.*

4. In sentence 5, replace *in the 18th and 19th centuries* with *over the next few hundred years.*

5. Combine sentences 6 and 7; begin your new sentence with *although.*

6. Rewrite the clause beginning *there was* in your new sentence to use the present perfect.

7. Sentence 8 has a prepositional phrase that indicates time. Move it to the beginning of the sentence because it is common in academic writing to have a phrase or clause before the subject of the main clause.

8. In sentence 9, replace *the airplane* with *their invention* to improve cohesion between sentences 8 and 9.

9. In sentence 11, replace *airplanes* with another word or phrase that conveys the same idea.

10. At the end of the paragraph, add a sentence that begins: *However, this ability to fly anywhere at anytime means that . . .* and complete the sentence with a negative result or drawback.

ACTIVITY 9 Original Writing

On a separate sheet of paper, write a descriptive or narrative paragraph (at least seven sentences) about an invention that interests you. Explain what it is and give facts, details, and examples. Use two or more examples of present perfect and underline them.

Here are some examples of how to begin.

- *One invention that has changed modern life is the cell phone.*
- *One of the most important inventions of the 20th century was the computer.*
- *Modern life is very different because of air conditioning.*

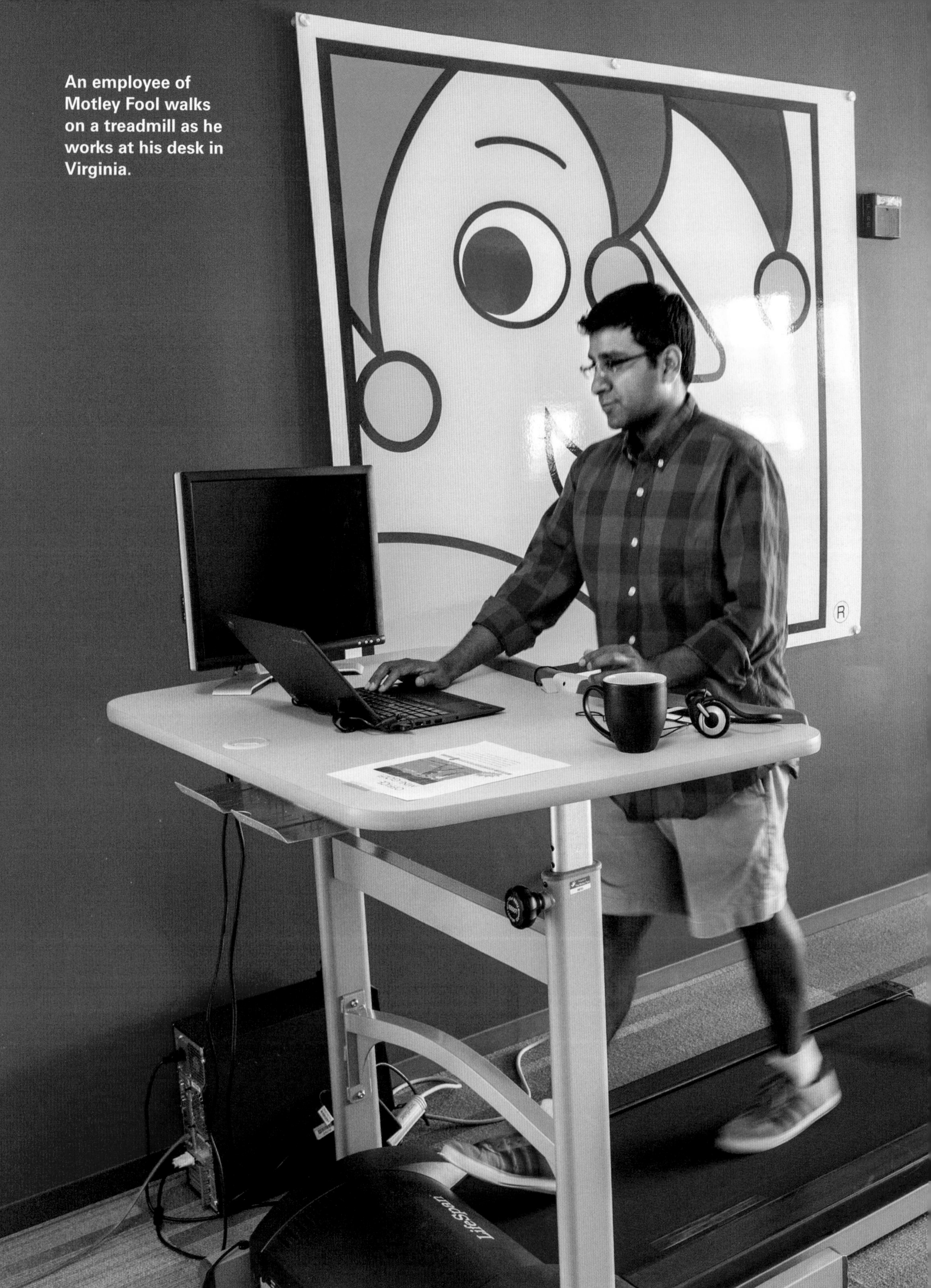

An employee of Motley Fool walks on a treadmill as he works at his desk in Virginia.

4 Using Word Forms

WHAT DO YOU KNOW?

DISCUSS Look at the photo and read the caption. Discuss the questions.

1. Where is the man? What is he doing? Why?
2. On average, how many hours do you spend sitting down each day?

FIND THE ERRORS This paragraph contains two errors with word forms. Find the errors and correct them. Explain your corrections to a partner.

CAUSE–EFFECT PARAGRAPH

The Dangers of Sitting

[1] People who spend too much time sitting down may be endangering their health, according to doctors at the Mayo Clinic. [2] Sit for extended periods of time—in front of a TV, behind a desk, or in a car—increases the risk of obesity, heart disease, high blood pressure, high cholesterol, and even death. [3] In one study, people who spent more than four hours a day in a chair had a greater chance of dying prematurely than those who spent less than two hours a day sitting down. [4] To offset these negative effects, doctors recommend less sitting and more moving. [5] Simple changes could include the following:

- [6] standing up while talking on the phone or watching TV
- [7] walking with colleagues instead of holding meetings in a conference room
- [8] installing a stand-up desk or placing one's computer on top of a counter or on a stand above a treadmill

[9] By moving more and sitting less, individuals can gain important benefits such as weight loss, increased energy, and more efficiency use of fats and sugars by the body. [10] All of these contribute to better overall health and a longer life.

Grammar Forms

4.1 Word Forms

In English, most words have different forms, which are associated with different parts of speech. Word endings (suffixes) usually indicate the part of speech of a word.

Part of Speech	Common Suffixes	Examples
Noun	*-tion*	*generation, inspiration, relation*
	-ity	*creativity, sensitivity, relativity*
	-ing	*enduring, singing, understanding* (gerunds)
	-ism	*communism, nationalism, realism*
	-ment	*disagreement, management, movement*
	-ness	*cheerfulness, happiness, illness*
Verb	*-ize*	*apologize, realize, visualize*
	-en	*darken, frighten, threaten*
	-ate	*animate, legislate, populate*
	-(i)fy	*classify, liquefy, verify*
Adjective	*-al*	*geographical, natural, original*
	-ed	*attached, revised, classified*
	-ent	*confident, efficient, innocent*
	-ive	*cooperative, creative, destructive*
	-ous	*dangerous, mountainous, venomous*
	-ate	*separate, fortunate, desperate*
	-ful	*successful, peaceful, powerful*
	-less	*careless, endless, useless*
Adverb	*-ly*	*extremely, rarely, likely, happily*

ACTIVITY 1

Identify the part of speech of the academic words. Write *noun*, *verb*, *adj* (adjective), or *adv* (adverb).

1. eventually ______________________

2. crucial ______________________

3. awareness ______________________

4. modify ______________________

5. contextualize ______________________

6. authority ______________________

7. administrative ______________________

8. racism ______________________

9. coherent ______________________

10. assessment ______________________

Common Uses

4.2 Using Word Forms

Nouns

1. Nouns formed from verbs or adjectives are very common in academic writing.	English is **difficult** for many learners to pronounce. One source of the **difficulty** is the complex system of English vowels (*from adjective, difficult*).
2. The most common noun suffix is *-tion*. Often a noun with *-tion* comes from a verb and means *act of* or *state of* the verb.	In 2012, the most frequently performed surgical **operation** was knee arthroplasty, meaning the replacement of a damaged joint (*operation = act of operating*).
3. Gerunds as subjects and as objects of prepositions are extremely common in academic writing.	**Singing** has both physical and mental benefits.

Verbs

1. The most common suffixes are: *-ize*, *-ate*, *-(i)fy*, and *-en*. They mean *become* or *cause to be*.	DNA can be used to **identify** both criminals and victims of crimes.
2. Verbs with these suffixes are often used in academic writing to describe processes or cause–effect relationships.	In an art appreciation class, students view slides of paintings that **exemplify** a particular style, period, or artist.

Adjectives and adverbs

1. Adjectives are used to describe nouns. The most common suffixes are: *-al*, *-ent*, *-ive*, *-ous*.	For patients at risk, doctors recommend an **annual** screening for skin cancer. Data showed a decrease in **violent** crime in 2014.
2. Adverbs modify verbs, adjectives, and other adverbs. The most common suffix for adverbs is *-ly*, which can add the meaning *in the manner of*.	It is recommended that patients visit their doctors at least twice **annually**. In nature, predators often attack their prey **violently**.

ACTIVITY 2

Fill in the blank with the correct form from each word family.

1. ________________ therapies are available for the treatment of phobias like fear of heights. (*Various / Variation / Variably*)

2. Astronomers ________________ that a mysterious force known as *dark energy* is causing the universe to expand. (*theorize / theoretical / theoretically*)

3. Scientists have successfully engineered artificial bone marrow that can produce both red and white blood cells ________________ . (*continuous / continuation / continuously*)

4. Dr. Dina Krasikova, an expert on leadership, writes that " ________________ flourishes in supportive environments where leaders and subordinates have good interpersonal relationships." (*create / creativity / creatively*)

5. The magazine *U.S. News & World Report* rated the 2016 Honda Civic as the most ________________ car in the United States. (*economize / economical / economically*)

6. The fight-or-flight ________________ is the body's natural and automatic reaction to both real and perceived danger. (*responsive / response / responsively*)

7. Research has shown ________________ that early exposure to more than one language is beneficial to a child's developing brain. (*consistency / consistent / consistently*)

8. Negative criticism hurts people's feelings and may cause resentment. On the other hand, ________________ criticism, which acknowledges people's strengths while focusing on specific behaviors that can be improved, motivates people to grow and change. (*construction / constructive / constructively*)

9. If there is a sudden drop in cabin pressure and the oxygen masks drop down, airline passengers are instructed to place the masks over their mouths and breathe ________________ . (*normal / normalize / normally*)

10. While the respondent was very ________________, she had trouble understanding when people were being sarcastic. (*perceptively / perceptive / perception*)

Common Errors

Common Error 4.1 Is the word form correct?

Thomas Jefferson believed that educated citizens were the basis of a ~~success~~ successful democracy.

REMEMBER: In English, the ending of a word often determines its part of speech. Omitting a suffix or using the wrong suffix changes the part of speech and is an error that could make the sentence difficult for the reader to understand.

ACTIVITY 3 Common Error 4.1

Read each sentence. Underline the correct word form in parentheses.

1. Sales of printed dictionaries have dropped as more and more readers have begun using apps to find a quick (*define / definition*) of a word.
2. Fats that are solid at room temperature, such as butter, (*liquefy / liquid*) when heated.
3. Self-driving cars have features that allow the car to brake, accelerate, and steer (*automation / automatically*).
4. Based on research conducted between 2007 and 2014, the Pew Research Center concluded that Americans are becoming less (*religious / religion*).
5. People who are accustomed to taking care of themselves worry about becoming (*dependence / dependent*) on others as they grow older.
6. Because horses are large and unpredictable, some people claim that horse (*rider / riding*) is one of the most dangerous sports in the world.
7. In this workshop, we intend to (*demonstrate / demonstration*) seven activities to help develop students' reading fluency.
8. Due to their hardness, diamonds have a wide variety of (*industry / industrial*) uses.
9. Researchers often caution that it is too soon to (*generally / generalize*) the results of experiments performed on animals to human populations.
10. Nonnative animal species, such as boa constrictors in the Florida Everglades, often (*threaten / threatening*) native species because they have no natural enemies to control their populations.

Common Error 4.2 Do you have the correct suffix?

development
The ~~developing~~ of a new vaccine is usually a long and costly process.

REMEMBER: Using the wrong suffix will make your sentence hard to understand.

ACTIVITY 4 Common Error 4.2

Read each sentence. The underlined words have incorrect suffixes. Write the correct word form above the word.

1. Samuel Morse, the inventor of Morse Code, gave the simplest codes to the most frequency occurring letters in the English alphabet.

2. In recent years, an ideologic tension has developed between extreme left and extreme right political parties in many countries.

3. The Americans with Disabilities Act of 1990, which forbids discrimination against people with disabilities, requires all sidewalks to be accessibility to people in wheelchairs.

4. Labels on medicine bottles specific how often patients should take the prescribed medicine.

5. In some large cities, the fine for parking illegal can be $300 or even more.

6. Almost all religions have a story that describes the creative of the world.

7. By analyze 2,000-year-old garbage found in a Roman tunnel, archeologists learned that the ancient Romans had a diverse diet that included fish, meat, vegetables, and fruit.

8. Many parenting books point out that it is good to let children experience the natural consequently of their own behavior. For example, if a child refuses to eat, let her get hungry.

Academic Vocabulary

Words with Common Suffixes Frequently Used in Academic Writing

community	creativity	finally	mechanism	section
consistent	emphasize	individual (adj)	positive	strengthen

Source: *Longman grammar of spoken and written English* (Biber, et al. 1999).

ACTIVITY 5 Vocabulary in Academic Writing

Use the academic vocabulary to complete the sentences.

Subject Area	Example from Academic Writing
Health	**1.** A recent study at Brigham Young University showed that going to bed and getting up at the same time each day were associated with lower body fat. This finding was __________________ with earlier research.
Education	**2.** In *Teaching and Researching Reading* (2011) Stoller and Grabe __________________ the importance of teaching reading strategies to students and giving students frequent opportunities to practice strategy use.
Music	**3.** The sonata, a type of classical music composition, typically has three __________________: exposition, development, and recapitulation.
Chemistry	**4.** Arsenic, an extremely powerful chemical used for killing rats, is known to cause cancer, but researchers have not been able to determine the precise __________________ by which it causes the disease.
Art and Literature	**5.** Some people theorize that __________________ and mental illness often go hand in hand. Artists such as Vincent Van Gogh and Sylvia Plath are examples.
Physiology	**6.** For patients with lower back pain, therapists recommend doing exercises that __________________ the core abdominal muscles, or abs.
Government	**7.** The United States Bill of Rights contains a number of __________________ liberties that by law cannot be taken away by the government.
Psychology	**8.** In 1938, B. F. Skinner introduced the concept of __________________ reinforcement, which means rewarding a desired behavior so that it will be repeated.
History	**9.** After declining in power for more than a hundred years, the western Roman Empire __________________ fell to Germanic conquerors in the year 476 CE.
Education	**10.** A learning __________________ is a group of concerned people who work together to create the best possible learning environment for a school or group of students.

Put It Together

ACTIVITY 6 Review Quiz

Multiple Choice Choose the letter of the correct answer.

1. Scientists using computer simulation software to _____ the bite of a giant prehistoric shark, *Megalodon*, found that the shark's bite was more powerful than that of a *T. rex* dinosaur.

   a. analyze **b.** analysis **c.** analytic **d.** analyst

2. Among most species of birds, it is up to the female to _____ a male that will assure the health of her babies.

   a. selective **b.** selection **c.** select **d.** selectively

3. In these insecure financial times, mutual funds can provide a more _____ source of retirement income than savings accounts or bonds.

   a. rely **b.** reliable **c.** reliance **d.** reliably

4. The modern age of weather _____ began with the invention of the telegraph in 1835.

   a. predict **b.** predictable **c.** predictably **d.** prediction

5. Does listening to classical music improve spatial-temporal reasoning? _____, does listening to the music of Wolfgang Amadeus Mozart have this effect?

   a. Specific **b.** Specify **c.** Specifically **d.** Specification

Error Correction One of the five underlined words or phrases is not correct. Find the error and correct it. Be prepared to explain your answer.

6. Communism is a way of organize society in which there is no private property and there are no social classes.

7. The word *gypsy* is a derogatory name for the Romani people, who originated in northern India but immigrated to Europe more than 1,500 years ago. The Romani original practiced the Hindu religion but today follow either Islam or Christianity.

8. Rubella is an infectious disease caused by the rubella virus. Normally the disease is not danger, but it can cause serious health problems for babies whose mothers catch it during pregnancy. A vaccine to prevent the disease was first introduced in 1969.

A magnificent old walnut tree stands on a farm in Maryland.

ACTIVITY 7 Building Greater Sentences

Combine these short sentences into one sentence. You can add new words and move words around, but you should not add or omit any ideas. More than one answer is possible, but all of these sentences include a variety of word forms.

1. **a.** Walnuts are extremely high in omega-3 fats.
   b. Walnuts are extremely high in antioxidants.
   c. Walnuts are an important part of our diet.
   d. This has been true for thousands of years.

2. **a.** Franz Boaz was a German-American anthropologist.
   b. He opposed an ideology called *scientific racism*.
   c. The ideology stated that race is biologically determined.

3. **a.** The world community sent Japan billions of dollars in aid.
   b. The aid was humanitarian.
   c. The aid followed the earthquake.
   d. The earthquake was in 2011.

ACTIVITY 8 Steps to Composing

Read the essay. Then follow the directions in the 10 steps to edit the information and composition of the essay. Write your revised paragraphs on a separate sheet of paper. Be careful with punctuation and capitalization. Check your answers with the class.

SUMMARY–RESPONSE ESSAY

Functional Textiles

[1] High-tech or functional textiles are synthetic fabrics with sensors and microchips built into them. [2] Steve Lohr wrote in the *New York Times* on April 1, 2016. [3] Steve Lohr describes an exciting new collaboration among U.S. universities, textile companies, and the Defense Department to create fabrics that can "see, hear, communicate, store energy, warm or cool a person, or monitor the wearer's health."

[4] High-tech fabrics could have useful applications in many areas. [5] For example, sports clothing that could be programmed could sense if a person is having a heart attack and then call for help. [6] Soldiers' uniforms could signal when an enemy is near and become invisible. [7] Mattresses could monitor a person's sleep and health.

[8] Functional fabrics could help to revive the struggling U.S. textile industry. [9] It has lost jobs as a result of the way the world has become more global. [10] Lohr writes that functional fabrics could "push the American textile industry into the digital age." [11] They could create thousands of new jobs in the process.

[12] The author cautions that many questions remain about the cost, design, marketing, and use of functional fabrics. [13] Critics worry about privacy and it is possible that the textiles could be hacked, like any digital product. [14] However, I am convinced that functional textiles have big potential to help solve real-world problems and to reinvigorate the U.S. textile industry.

1. Change sentence 2 to a participial phrase beginning with *Writing*. Delete *Steve Lohr*. Then combine sentences 2 and 3.
2. Summaries should include attribution to the author of the original piece. Insert *According to Lohr* at the beginning of sentence 4.
3. Sometimes a word with a suffix can replace an entire phrase or clause. This makes your writing less wordy. In sentence 5, replace *that could be programmed* with the adjective *programmable*. Place the adjective before *sports clothing*.
4. Transitions make writing more coherent. In sentence 8, add *In addition* or *Also*.
5. Combine sentences 8 and 9. Change sentence 9 into an adjective clause beginning with a comma and *which*.
6. In sentence 9, reduce wordiness by replacing *the way the world has become more global* with the noun *globalization*.
7. Combine sentences 10 and 11 by reducing sentence 11 to a verb phrase.
8. In sentence 12, replace *use* with *usability*.
9. In sentence 13, to improve parallel structure, change the phrase *it is possible* to a noun form starting with *the*.
10. In sentence 14, replace *big* with a more powerful word like *tremendous* or *enormous*.

ACTIVITY 9 Original Writing

On a separate piece of paper, write a summary–response paragraph (at least seven sentences) about a recent product or development in the high-tech field. Underline the nouns, verbs, adjectives, and adverbs with suffixes. Include source information.

Here are some examples of how to begin.

- *In a product review on cnet.com dated April 17, 2016, Xiomara Blanca reviews the advantages and disadvantages of the new HP Stream laptop.*
- *Writing in the April 11, 2016, issue of* Scientific American, *author Larry Greenemeier discusses Facebook's plan to install "chatbots" in the new version of its Messenger platform.*
- *The editorial "Welcome to the Drone Age" appeared in the September 26, 2015, issue of* The Economist. *In this article, the writer talks about the explosion in the use of drones in the United States.*

A computer-generated image shows influenza viruses in the airways of the lungs.

5 Writing with Prepositions

WHAT DO YOU KNOW?

DISCUSS Look at the photo and read the caption. Discuss the questions.

1. How is influenza (the flu) spread from person to person?
2. What can you do to stay healthy during the flu season?

FIND THE ERRORS This paragraph contains two errors with prepositions. Find the errors and correct them. Explain your corrections to a partner.

PROCESS PARAGRAPH

Your Immune System

[1] How does the human immune system fight infection and disease? [2] Infection is caused by pathogens. [3] A pathogen is a substance that your body identifies as harmful. [4] It can be a virus, bacteria, or even pollen. [5] On the outside on the cell of the pathogen are antigens, usually pieces of protein. [6] Your immune system relies by white blood cells to fight these outside threats. [7] The white blood cells recognize the antigens as the enemy and begin to multiply. [8] During this initial response period, infections usually worsen, making you feel sick. [9] However, within a few days, your body is often able to defend itself. [10] Some white blood cells (lymphocytes) produce antibodies which weaken the pathogen. [11] Other cells (phagocytes) actually eat the pathogen. [12] If the immune system is weak, or if the number of pathogens in the body is very high, it may be difficult to fight the infection.

Grammar Forms

5.1 Prepositions

Type	Example	Example Sentence
Single-word Prepositions	*of, to, in, for, with, on, at, from, about, after, before, between, by, since, without, near*	One reason **for** the increase **in** traffic is the growing economy in the area.
Multi-word Prepositions	*because of, regardless of, due to, across from, in place of, in spite of, with regard to*	Fewer companies are opening offices in this state **because of** recent restrictions. **In spite of** the recent turmoil in international markets, the U.S. economy has remained surprisingly strong.

5.2 Prepositional Phrases

Type	Example Sentence
1. Preposition + noun phrase	Many tourists visit Washington, D.C., **in the spring**.
2. Preposition + object pronoun (*me, you, him, her, it, us, them*)	Visitors to New York City find the subway is easy **for them to use**.
3. Preposition + gerund	If you are interested **in attending the World Cup**, there are a few things to keep in mind.
4. Preposition + *wh-* clause	Here are some tips **about what you should do in Paris**.

Notes

1. Prepositional phrases can occur in the beginning, in the middle, or at the end of a sentence. In academic writing, it is common to begin a sentence with a prepositional phrase followed by a comma.
   In the spring, many tourists visit Washington, D.C.
2. A prepositional phrase between the subject and the verb does not usually affect the verb form.
   S V
   The effects **of climate change** are obvious.
   S V
   The effects **of increasing temperatures** are obvious.
3. The object of the preposition is the noun, pronoun, gerund, phrase or clause that follows the preposition.
4. *To* + noun (*to the office*) is a prepositional phrase, but to + verb (*to take*) is an infinitive.

ACTIVITY 1

For each sentence, underline the preposition and the object of the preposition. There are two or more in each sentence.

1. An interest rate refers to the amount of money, usually a percentage of the total, that you have to pay when you borrow from a bank or other lending institution.
2. When the price of oil drops, it can be more economical to make new materials, including plastic, rather than recycle materials from garbage.
3. Under a law passed in 1966, Cubans who set foot on U.S. soil are allowed to remain and are eligible for government benefits.
4. When your cell phone is low on power and you are running errands around town, you might recharge one day simply by plugging your phone into your shoe.
5. One way property owners can reduce the use of water in dry climates is to switch from lawns to native grasses and plants with a greater drought tolerance.
6. You can reduce cholesterol levels by switching to a vegan diet and exercising for at least 30 minutes a day.
7. Chinese shoppers often take daylong cruises to western Japan to shop for clothes and electronics because of the lower prices and better quality there.
8. In the Great Backyard Bird Count, thousands of bird-watchers flock to parks and other outdoor spaces to sit and count birds for at least 15 minutes and then upload their findings to a database.

Common Uses

5.3 Preposition Use: Function

Prepositions are used to show the relationship between two nouns (nouns, noun phrases, noun clauses, or gerunds). *The salmon swim* ***up*** *the river every year.* Prepositions are used to show relationships involving:

1. location	**in** Antarctica **on** 9th Street	**near** Chile **by** the river	**at** work **above** the atmosphere
2. time	**at** night **in** 2015 **before** noon	**since** the recession **for** two decades **after** 5 p.m.	**on** July 20 **in** the evening **during** the night
3. direction or movement	**to** Pakistan **from** Canada	**along** the highway **up** Mt. Everest	**into** trouble **down** the cliff
4. the manner or way of doing something	The work was not completed **according to** the contract. More sunlight was gained **by** cutting down the trees.		
5. cause and effect or problem and solution	Families began to relocate **because of** the air pollution. His idea **resulted in** greater profits. Store canned food **in case of** a disaster.		
6. Prepositional phrases also give more information about a noun.	Visitors **without an invitation** were not permitted to enter. Support **for the conservative candidates** has increased dramatically.		

5.4 Preposition Use: Combinations

Prepositions occur in collocations (common word combinations) and regularly come after certain verbs, nouns, and adjectives. Using collocations correctly is important in academic writing.

Verbs

account for	People in China and India **account for** half of the world's population living with water scarcity.
deal with	The report **deals with** preventing and treating diabetes.
depend on	Your risk for certain diseases **depends on** both environmental and genetic factors.
focus on	This paper will **focus on** explaining the process of photosynthesis.

Verbs (Continued)

look for / at	In *Outliers,* Malcolm Gladwell **looked at** factors that influence success.
participate in	The students who **participated in** the study were placed in one of two groups.
provide for	The budget **provides for** a new arts program.
range from	Significant stressors **range from** changing jobs to experiencing the death of a family member.
result in / from	The new testing requirements **result in** increased dropout rates.

Adjectives

associated with	In a recent study greater happiness was **associated with** spending money on things that fit your personality.
compared to / with	The Dutch are getting taller more quickly **compared to** Americans and most other Europeans.
familiar with	Research shows that people often like things just because they are **familiar with** them.
involved in	Older adults who are **involved in** community activities are often healthier, both mentally and physically, than more isolated adults.
related to	Stress may be **related to** late-night snacking according to a recent Norwegian study.
responsible for	Scientists suspect that evolution may be **responsible for** the increased height of the Dutch.
similar to	Children often pursue careers that are **similar to** those of their parents.

Nouns

the effects of	**The effects of** coal mining have been devastating.
an impact on	*To Kill a Mockingbird* had **an impact on** my view of racial relationships in the American South.
a lack of	Autism is often characterized by **an** apparent **lack of** empathetic feeling.
the percent of	**The percent of** Americans living without health insurance has decreased. It has fallen to 9.1 percent.
the reason for	Experts cite the availability of guns as **the reason for** the increase in shooting deaths.
the relationship between	Research suggests **the relationship between** happiness and spending money may be complicated.
understanding of	The article increased our **understanding of** how ice sheets behave.

ACTIVITY 2

Read each sentence. Underline the correct preposition in parentheses.

1. People who are involved (*for / in*) certain kinds (*for / of*) focused activities often report being in a state (*of / with*) flow, or increased energy.
2. Some politicians still question the existence (*in / of*) a causal relationship (*between / with*) human activity and climate change.
3. (*In / On*) December 1911, Roald Amundsen was the first person to reach the South Pole, arriving (*at / in*) his destination just one month (*before / since*) Robert Scott.
4. In today's workforce, companies are looking (*for / of*) employees (*of / with*) experience (*in / on*) problem-solving and teamwork.
5. Water evaporates (*above / into*) the atmosphere, leading (*for / to*) the development (*of / with*) clouds, which get heavier and heavier until water falls back (*at / to*) the earth (*in / with*) the form (*of / on*) precipitation.
6. When you read online, you cannot focus (*on / with*) the text as well as you can (*at / with*) print.
7. Due (*of / to*) the severe flooding, the state suffered economic losses (*at / in*) the neighborhood of $400 million.
8. Symptoms associated (*from / with*) the flu can often linger (*for / to*) as long as 10 days.
9. People who participate (*on / in*) insider trading should be prosecuted. They use their inside knowledge (*at / of*) markets to make investments. Insider trading results (*in / with*) a loss of $1.75 trillion globally.
10. According (*with / to*) a recent survey, 83 percent (*of / at*) women do household chores as compared (*for / with*) 65 percent (*of / at*) men.

Common Errors

Common Error 5.1 Which preposition is correct?

At some point ~~on~~ in the 21st century, humans will establish a colony in outer space.

REMEMBER: Prepositions occur with certain collocations. Make sure you use the correct preposition.

ACTIVITY 3 **Common Error 5.1**

Fill in the blank with the correct preposition from the box. Some prepositions may be used more than once.

about	at	for	in	on
as	between	from	of	with

1. Tremors are associated ______________ some neurological conditions such as Parkinson's. A tremor usually involves shaking ______________ the hands or face.
2. They interviewed 100 students who served ______________ peer counselors and asked them ______________ their experiences. The results ______________ the interviews are displayed ______________ Table 3.1.
3. Students who are interested ______________ pursuing a major ______________ psychology need to take 30 hours ______________ classes in that area.
4. Living ______________ a dorm is very different ______________ living ______________ home. ______________ one thing, you share your space ______________ many strangers.
5. ______________ the numbers ______________ older adults increasing every year, it is important that we have an understanding ______________ how to help them remain healthy as long as possible. Older adults who engage ______________ aerobic exercises ______________ a regular basis benefit ______________ workouts ______________ several ways.
6. ______________ this paper, I will talk ______________ the relationship ______________ violent behavior and video games.

Common Error 5.2 Do you have a noun form after the preposition?

Due to water ~~restricted~~ restrictions, homeowners are not allowed to water their lawns.

Economists are worried about ~~increase~~ increasing the interest rate during a recession.

REMEMBER: Use only nouns, noun phrases, or noun clauses after a preposition. Do not use a verb; use a gerund.

ACTIVITY 4 Common Error 5.2

Fill in the blank with the correct form of the word in parentheses. Some nouns may need plural forms.

1. Even babies are capable of ________________ (*judge*) the likelihood of certain events.
2. Biologists worry about ________________ (*endanger*) other species through human behavior.
3. The benefits of ________________ (*do*) yoga include relaxation and improved balance.
4. Professors familiar with the ________________ (*concern*) of students should advocate for them with the administration.
5. The FIFA officials involved in ________________ (*take*) bribes faced a variety of consequences—from criminal indictment to loss of their positions.
6. Because of ________________ (*change*) in health insurance requirements, the uninsured face penalties.
7. Consistent with the ________________ (*result*) of last year's survey, we found that women perform more household chores than men.
8. Politicians need to have a basic understanding of ________________ (*negotiate*).

Common Error 5.3 Does the main verb of the sentence agree with the subject?

The most frequent complaint (S) of retail customers (PP) ~~are~~ is (V) regarding service.

Tourists (S) from Japan (PP) often ~~visits~~ visit (V) Washington, D.C., in the spring.

REMEMBER: The verb should agree with the main noun in the subject, not the noun in an intervening prepositional phrase.

ACTIVITY 5 Common Error 5.3

In each set of sentences, fill in the blank with the correct form of the verbs in parentheses.

1. Using a device for monitoring blood sugar levels ______________________ (*be*, simple present) very important to patients with diabetes. The frequency of such checks ______________________ (*depend*, simple present) on the type of diabetes the patient has.

2. Phones without Wi-Fi capability ______________________ (*decline*, present progressive) in popularity these days. The current median rate of smartphone ownership ______________________ (*be*, simple present) 68 percent in advanced economies and 37 percent in emerging and developing economies.

3. Artifacts found on the shore of Easter Island ______________________ (*turn out*, present perfect) to be general purpose tools rather than spear points as was originally thought. This suggests that perhaps the people in this island society ______________________ (*be*, simple past) not destroyed by war.

4. In the video for Beyonce's "Formation," images of post-Katrina New Orleans ______________________ (*provide*, simple present) the setting for her song that ______________________ (*address*, simple present) issues related to being black in the modern day United States.

5. A report on poverty in developing countries ______________________ (*state*, simple present) that there has been a gradual reduction in recent years. However, many developed countries, including the United States, ______________________ (*show*, simple present) a growing disparity in wealth.

6. According to recent reports, the unpaid work of women ______________________ (*have*, simple present) hidden costs. The time spent on chores and childcare ______________________ (*mean*, simple present) that women are less likely to go to school or join the workforce.

Academic Vocabulary

Preposition Combinations Frequently Used in Academic Writing

associated with	difference between	lack of	reason for	support for
consistent with	due to	need for	responsible for	used to

Source: Corpus of Contemporary American English (Davies 2008–)

ACTIVITY 6 Vocabulary in Academic Writing

Underline the correct word in parentheses and fill in the correct preposition.

Subject Area	Example from Academic Writing
Education	**1.** Lower achievement in school can often be traced to a (*support / lack*) ______________ parental involvement.
Political Science	**2.** Certain characteristics are (*reason / associated*) ______________ a tendency to vote. People who are older and better educated are more likely to vote than younger, less educated people.
Environmental Science	**3.** The results of a recent study demonstrate a (*difference / need*) ______________ policies that will protect pollinators like birds and bees.
Sociology	**4.** The (*supports / reasons*) ______________ the increase in violent crime in the area include poverty, gang activity, and the greater availability of guns.
History	**5.** The congresswoman's (*due / support*) ______________ the new farm bill was surprising.
Health	**6.** The researchers' findings are (*consistent / responsible*) ______________ those of earlier studies—weight-bearing exercise promotes bone strength.
Economics	**7.** Problematic lending practices were (*responsible / reason*) ______________ the collapse of the housing market in 2007 and 2008.
English Composition	**8.** One significant (*need / difference*) ______________ the United States and other developed countries is the frequency of mass shootings.
Nursing	**9.** Doctors and patients have become (*used / responsible*) ______________ relying on antibiotics to treat illness.
International Relations	**10.** The strength of the relationship between the United States and Great Britain is in part (*consistent / due*) ______________ their shared history and language.

Put It Together

ACTIVITY 7 Review Quiz

Multiple Choice Choose the letter of the correct answer.

1. Researchers have long suspected a relationship ______ obesity and processed food.

   a. about **b.** between **c.** in **d.** of

2. World leaders have been meeting in Brussels ______ the last two days to discuss the crisis in Africa.

   a. at **b.** for **c.** in **d.** on

3. Voters signaled their support ______ greater restrictions on immigration and increased border security.

   a. for **b.** of **c.** to **d.** with

4. According to recent research, a high level ______ productivity is associated with teams who show empathy for each other and allow everyone to speak for an equal amount of time.

   a. between **b.** for **c.** of **d.** with

5. In Paris, an ambitious plan ______ a revitalized subway system may help solve a number of societal problems.

   a. at **b.** by **c.** except **d.** for

Error Correction One of the five underlined words or phrases is not correct. Find the error and correct it. Be prepared to explain your answer.

6. <u>In</u> the beginning <u>of</u> the 20th century, Americans benefited <u>for</u> increased industrialization even <u>as</u> they experienced some <u>of</u> its negative consequences.

7. <u>As</u> part <u>of</u> the study, participants listened <u>to</u> music <u>of</u> 20 minutes <u>before</u> completing a task.

8. A relatively small number <u>of</u> American students are excelling <u>at</u> math <u>in</u> world competitions although you would not know it <u>by</u> looking <u>on</u> national test scores overall.

ACTIVITY 8 Building Greater Sentences

Combine these short sentences into one sentence. You can add new words and move words around, but you should not add or omit any ideas. More than one answer is possible, but all of these sentences require prepositional phrases.

1. **a.** Researchers estimate some Americans are exposed to harmful noise.
b. Their estimate is one-third of Americans.
c. The researchers are at the University of Michigan.
d. Those Americans might be at risk of health problems.
e. The problems are noise-related.

____

____

2. **a.** Dan Grunspan is an anthropologist.
b. He works at the University of Washington.
c. There is gender bias in the classroom.
d. Dan Grunspan decided to quantify the degree of the bias.
e. His colleagues at the University of Washington and elsewhere decided to quantify the degree of bias.

____

____

3. **a.** There are roughly 7,000 languages spoken on Earth.
b. Nearly half will likely disappear.
c. This will happen by the next century.
d. Communities abandon native tongues.
e. They speak English, Mandarin, or Spanish instead.

____

____

ACTIVITY 9 Steps to Composing

Read the paragraph. Then follow the directions in the 10 steps to edit the information and composition of the paragraph. Write your revised paragraph on a separate sheet of paper. Be careful with capitalization and punctuation. Check your answers with the class.

PROBLEM–SOLUTION PARAGRAPH

How New York City Faced a Challenge

[1] U.S. cities are growing much more quickly than the suburbs. [2] Urban areas have increasingly become magnets for affluent and professional young adults. [3] However, they still face serious problems associated with high density, including crime, traffic, pollution, and housing shortages. [4] How effectively cities deal with these problems may determine how well they continue to be innovative places. [5] New York City is an example of a city that dealt effectively with the crime problem. [6] New York was perhaps the most dangerous city in the United States in the 1970s. [7] More violent crimes were committed on its public transportation than on any other transportation system in the world. [8] But the New York of today is relatively safe. [9] Something happened. [10] In 1990, the police department changed how it approached fighting crime. [11] They did not ignore things like graffiti and littering, and they decided to arrest people for even small crimes. [12] According to their theory, people were more likely to commit serious crimes if laws were not enforced. [13] Their strategy seemed to work. In three years, the number of crimes decreased drastically.

1. In sentence 1, change *more quickly* to *at a much more rapid rate.*
2. Join sentences 2 and 3 with *although* to show contrast.
3. In sentence 4, replace *innovative places* with *centers of innovation* for greater emphasis.
4. In sentence 5, change *crime problem* to *problem of crime.*
5. In sentence 6, to focus attention on the time, move *in the 1970s* to the beginning of the sentence.

6. In sentence 7, change *public transportation* to *subway trains.* This is more specific and does not use *transportation* twice in one sentence.
7. In sentence 8, replace *But* with *In contrast.*
8. Change sentence 9 to a question. Although you do not want to use them too often, questions can sometimes help engage the reader or emphasize a point.
9. In sentence 10, change *how it approached fighting crime* to a noun phrase starting with *its approach.* Academic writing uses more nouns than verbs.
10. Begin sentence 11 with *instead of.* You will have to make other changes in the sentence as well.

A man removes graffiti from a Graffiti Free NYC truck.

ACTIVITY 10 Original Writing

On a separate piece of paper, write a problem–solution paragraph (at least seven sentences) about a problem your city, community, or school faces and a possible solution. Use at least one example of a noun + preposition combination and one adjective + preposition combination and underline them; try to use two of each type if possible.

Here are some examples of how to begin.

- *One of the problems facing our city today is a shortage of affordable housing.*
- *Young adults face a variety of challenges when they graduate from college, including finding a job.*
- *Perhaps the most serious challenge students face today is bullying in school.*

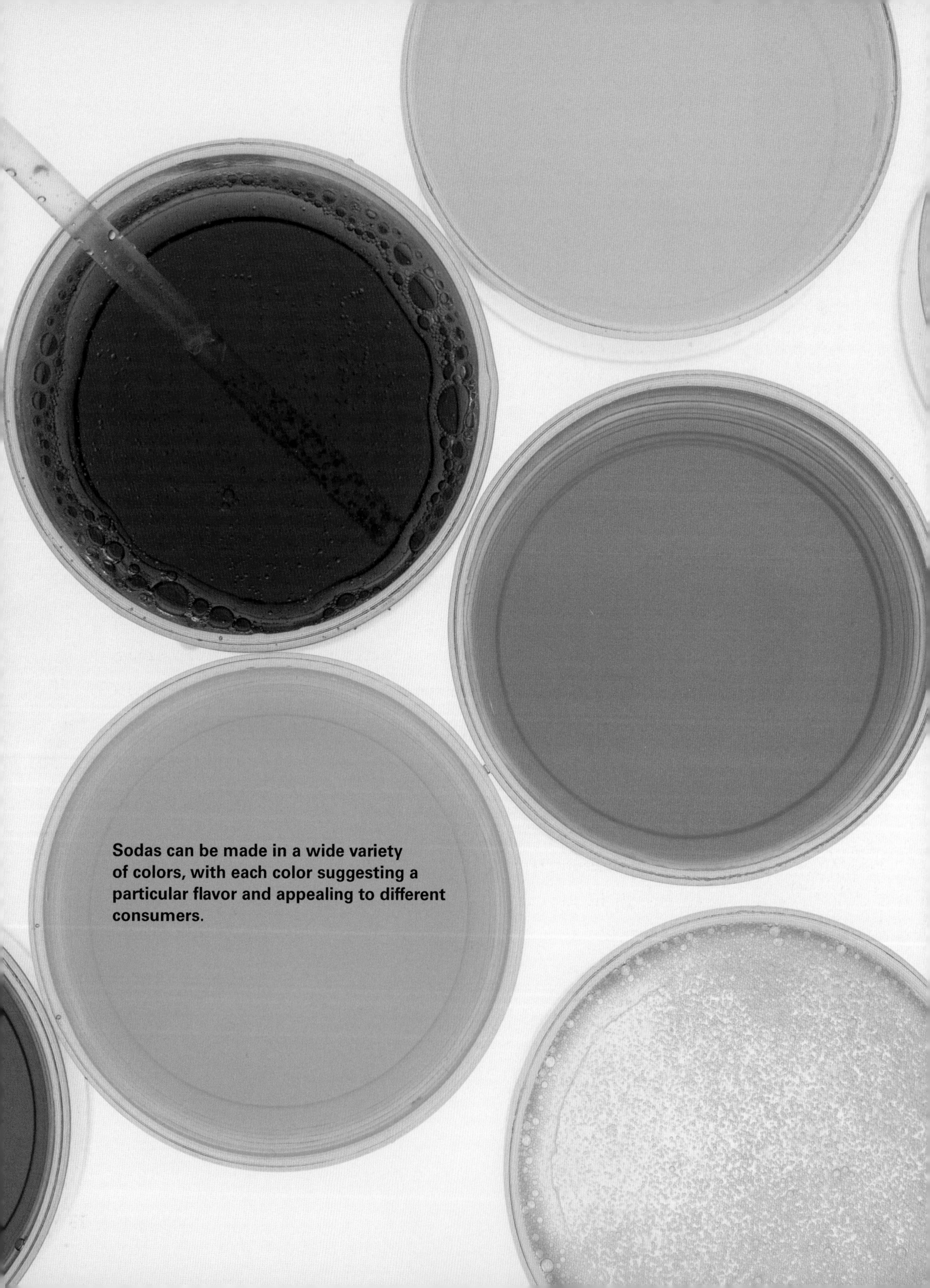

Sodas can be made in a wide variety of colors, with each color suggesting a particular flavor and appealing to different consumers.

6 Using Modals

WHAT DO YOU KNOW?

DISCUSS Look at the photo and read the caption. Discuss the questions.

1. Would you like to taste a drink with one of these colors? Which one? Why?
2. At what age should parents let children choose their own food and drinks?

FIND THE ERRORS This paragraph contains two errors with a modal. Find the errors and correct them. Explain one error and your correction to a partner.

CAUSE–EFFECT PARAGRAPH

Warning Labels on Sugar-Sweetened Drinks

[1] Studies have shown that drinks marketed specifically to children can contain more than six teaspoons of sugar. [2] As a result, these drinks are a major contributor to childhood obesity, juvenile diabetes, and tooth decay. [3] Researchers at the University of Pennsylvania School of Medicine were interested in finding out whether warning labels on sugary drinks, similar to warnings found on tobacco products, can to influence parents' decisions whether or not to buy sugar-sweetened drinks for their children. [4] The study concluded that parents at every level of education maybe less likely to buy sugary drinks if they contain health-warning labels. [5] An additional benefit of these labels is that they may help educate parents about the potential health problems caused by consuming too much sugar. [6] In fact, the U.S. Department of Agriculture now recommends that less than 10 percent of a child's diet should come from added sugar.

Grammar Forms

6.1 Modals

Modals use this pattern: modal + (*not* +) verb.

Modal	Example
can	In some cases, physical therapy **can be** more effective than surgery in reducing pain.
may	Future research **may not find** a better solution than the current one.
might	A snake bite is an example of a medical problem that **might require** hospital treatment.
could	In the future, humans **could live** on Mars. The surgeon **could not repair** the torn heart valve, but he was able to replace it.
will	This paper **will present** two new theories about President Kennedy's assassination.
would	A permanent solution to global warming **would** certainly **cost** billions of dollars.
should	The new manager **should not introduce** major changes right away.

Notes

1. Use the base form of the verb when it follows a modal. Do not use the infinitive.
2. For passive forms, use the base form of *be* and the past participle form of the main verb. (*A better solution **may not be found**. Hospital treatment **might be required**.*)
3. Do not confuse *maybe* and *may be*. *Maybe* is an adverb; *may be* is a modal + main verb. (***Maybe** the product **will be** available at the end of this month. The product **may be** available at the end of this month.)*

6.2 Phrasal Modals

Phrasal modals are multi-word expressions that are similar in meaning to one-word modals. Phrasal modals usually begin with a form of *be* or *have* and are followed by *to* + verb.

Modal	Example
(do not) have to + verb	By law, a person applying for a credit card **does not have to state** his or her race, religion, or ethnicity.
be (not) able to + verb	Doctors **were able to save** the life of the accident victim.
be (not) supposed to + verb	Given the length of the Web site's privacy statements, it seems the user **is not supposed to read** the content before agreeing.

Note

For passive forms, use phrasal modal + *to be* + past participle.

Your age **does not have to be stated** on the form.

The statement **is supposed to be read** by users before they sign it.

6.3 Past Modals

Past modals use this pattern: modal + (*not* +) *have* + past participle.

Modal	Example
might	The amount of water in the container **might have affected** the result of the experiment.
should	More people **should have voted** in the last election.
may	The students **may not have been** completely honest in their responses to the questionnaire.
could	Better hygiene **could have prevented** millions of deaths in the region.

Notes

1. In past modals, use modal + *have* + past participle for all singular and plural subjects.
2. The passive form of past modals is modal + *have been* + past participle.
   Many deaths **could have been prevented** by better hygiene.

ACTIVITY 1

Read each sentence. Underline the correct answer from the words in parentheses.

1. King Arthur is a fictional character, but he (*may be / maybe*) based on a real king who lived in England during the fifth or sixth century.
2. People with celiac disease (*is not able to / are not able to*) eat wheat in any form.
3. In the Roman Republic (509–27 BCE), women (*could not have / could not*) vote or hold public office.
4. A study commissioned by Samsung predicts that within 100 years, people (*could / will be*) able to travel through "skyways" in their own personal drones.
5. Detectives (*are supposed to / are supposed to be*) inform criminal suspects of their right to remain silent and their right to a lawyer before asking them any questions.
6. Criminal suspects (*are supposed to / are supposed to be*) informed of their right to remain silent and their right to a lawyer before they are asked any questions.
7. Patrons of the New York Public Library (*can be / can*) download more than 180,000 high-resolution images, including classic posters, for free.
8. Evidence suggests that a collision between the earth and a comet or meteor (*may have been / may have*) caused the extinction of the dinosaurs 65 million years ago.
9. Ancient Egypt's King Tut (*may / may have*) walked with a cane.
10. Experiments by researchers in the Netherlands using simulated Martian and moon soil (*could / could have*) lead to humans being able to grow crops in space someday.

Common Uses

6.4 Using Modals

Modals are used to add flavor or meaning to verbs.

1. Use *will* to state strong predictions or strong assertions.	
• Use *will* in the introduction to state your plan for organizing an essay or paper.	This paper **will examine** the effects of pollution on the Texas seafood industry.
• Use *will* to state strong predictions; this is common in the conclusion.	Within 20 years, our university's medical research facility **will become** a leader in the field.
• Use adverbs such as *probably* or *possibly* + *will* to weaken an assertion.	Employees who do not engage in continuing education **will probably find** their skills becoming obsolete.
2. Use *could* to indicate a present or future possibility or a past ability.	The island **could disappear** beneath the ocean within the next 50 years.
• Use *could not* to say someone or something was not able to do something, or that something was not possible in the past.	In the moonlight, we **could see** the baby sea turtles moving toward the ocean. Some of the sea turtles **could not climb** over mounds of sand, but volunteers helped them.
3. Use *must* or *have to* to express necessity or strong advisability.	In English, subjects **must agree** with verbs in person and number.
• *Did not have to* indicates a lack of necessity in the past, but *must not have* + past participal indicates an assumption about something.	Until 2006, airline passengers **did not have to remove** their shoes while going through an airport security check. The train conductor **must not have seen** the signal before the crash.
4. Use *should* for a situation that is advisable or recommended. • *Should* is not as strong as *must*.	Your teaching portfolio **should include** course outlines and examples of successful lessons or activities.
5. Use *was / were not able to* to express lack of ability in the past.	Firefighters **were not able to stop** the 2015 Valley Fire in Northern California from spreading.
6. Use *was / were not supposed to* to express an unanticipated action in the past.	Kennedy **was not supposed to defeat** Nixon in the 1960 presidential election—yet he did.

6.5 Using Modals for Hedging

In academic writing, one of the most common uses of modals is for *hedging*. Hedging means making a statement less assertive or less direct. Specific uses are as follows:

1. to make a statement less probable, certain, or assertive (*can, could, may, might*)	Experts fear that lions in Africa **could become** extinct. People who do not engage in continued education **may find** their skills quickly becoming obsolete.
2. to make a statement about the past sound less probable, certain, or assertive (*could / may / might* + *have* + past participle)	Psychologists speculate that many great artists, such as Vincent Van Gogh, **might have had** an illness.
3. to soften assertions or opinions that a reader might challenge (*would*) **a.** with *advocate, argue, assert, assume, claim, propose, suggest* **b.** with *it would seem / appear*	Recent data **would suggest** that Antarctic ice is melting faster than was previously expected. At this time, **it would seem** that a normalization of relations between the two countries is possible.
4. to hedge conclusions or predictions *(should)*	The patient's condition **should improve** following a 10-day course of antibiotics.
5. to modify a statement • common adverbs: *apparently, arguably, evidently, frequently, generally, likely, normally, partially, probably, possibly, roughly, surely, typically, usually*	The company's reasons for relocating the plant to the town **will likely be** of interest to the local residents.

Notes

1. Good academic writers hedge to protect themselves from the risk of error, to reduce the chance of opposition, and to report the limits of their findings. Hedge words and expressions are extremely important in all types of academic writing.
2. The phrases *I think* or *maybe* are infrequent in academic writing. Acceptable alternatives include *I would suggest . . .* and *It may be. . . .*

ACTIVITY 2

Complete the sentences with the modals from the box.

can	did not have to	may have	must not	were not supposed to
could	has to	have to	were able to	will

1. This paper ______________________ examine the life of Malcolm X, an American civil rights leader in the 1960s.
2. King Tut's mother ______________________ been one of his father's sisters. Researchers are not completely sure. The evidence ______________________ more definitively prove this theory.
3. Recent surveys show that high school ______________________ often be very stressful for students. Students ______________________ learn to let go of the stress. They ______________________ be afraid to talk to a counselor if their stress becomes unbearable.
4. Laptops started becoming mainstream in the 1990s, giving rise to increased mobility. An office worker ______________________ work in an office anymore. The laptop meant that a person ______________________ work anywhere.
5. Although some of the children in the 2002 study did eat the sweets, they ______________________. Some of them ______________________ control their impulses better than others.

ACTIVITY 3

For each set of sentences, underline the words and phrases used for hedging.

1. In a study, left-handed children performed worse on some tasks than right-handed ones, and mixed-handed kids performed worse than lefties. Nevertheless, it would appear that being left- or mixed-handed could not be seen as a predictor of a child's future success, the author of the study said.
2. In the near future, a test that relies on an analysis of a patient's breath could possibly be used to diagnose certain types of cancer.
3. In his book *How to Build a Time Machine*, the physicist Paul Davies says the theory of relativity would suggest that "a limited form" of time travel could probably happen. Moreover, it would seem that "unlimited" time travel—that is, travel to the past, present, or future—might be possible as well.
4. Life expectancy is increasing in the United States. As a result, demographers predict that costs related to health care and pensions will probably be higher than previous calculations may have indicated.
5. Author Terry Masear, who wrote a book about her work rescuing injured hummingbirds, says that the tiny birds can apparently experience post-traumatic stress syndrome (PTSD).

Common Errors

Common Error 6.1 Is the form of the modal correct?

This paper will ~~to~~ discuss the impact of outsourced textile factories on the economies of two Malaysian villages.

REMEMBER: Most modals do not use *to*. Only use *to* with forms of *have to, be able to,* or *be supposed to.*

ACTIVITY 4 Common Error 6.1

Correct the errors with *to* in the following sentences. Not all sentences will have corrections.

1. The world's fastest roller coaster, the Formula Rossa, can to travel at speeds up to 149 miles (240 km) per hour.
2. Someday soon, doctors may be able to perform surgery without cutting the skin.
3. Aspirin is effective against pain, but it may to cause an upset stomach in some people.
4. Travelers are not supposed to pack sharp objects in their carry-on luggage.
5. The *Juno* spacecraft will to orbit around the planet Jupiter for approximately 20 months.
6. If the earth's population continues to grow, we could to run out of clean water.
7. It is a myth that people are not supposed to go swimming after they eat.
8. People who have an unexplained fever for several days in a row should to see a doctor.

Common Error 6.2 Do you need a modal to hedge?

The Zika virus ~~is~~ may be responsible for the dramatic increase in the number of babies born with microcephaly.

REMEMBER: Hedge words and expressions are critical in academic writing. Academic writers almost never claim that their ideas are absolutely true.

ACTIVITY 5 **Common Error 6.2**

For each sentence, soften the strong assertion by adding the modal in parentheses. Make other changes to the sentence as needed.

1. (*can*) Without proper treatment, wounds become infected.

   ____

2. (*should*) The next version of a reusable space vehicle will be ready for launch in the next two years.

   ____

3. (*would*) The findings from a recent study suggest that milk protein is better than soy protein for building muscle mass in weight lifters.

   ____

4. (*may*) Students with special dietary or lifestyle needs prefer to live off campus.

   ____

5. (*could*) A discovery by Dr. Fraser Scott and colleagues at the University of Ottawa will lead to new treatments for diabetes.

   ____

6. (*may*) In the tech industry, women's coding work gets less respect than men's even though it is better.

   ____

7. (*might*) Americans traveling in Great Britain do not feel confident driving on the left side of the road.

   ____

8. (*should*) Staying up all night does not have an adverse effect on healthy young people.

   ____

Common Error 6.3 Do you use *I think* or *maybe* for hedging?

Autism could have
~~I think autism has~~ a genetic basis.

Autism may have
~~Maybe autism has~~ a genetic basis.

REMEMBER: *Maybe* and *I think* are rarely used in academic writing.

ACTIVITY 6 Common Error 6.3

Rewrite the sentences using the expressions in the box. Make other changes to the sentences as needed. More than one answer may be possible.

There may be	I would argue that
may look like	It could
it might be	I would suggest that
I would predict that	may have been

1. Maybe there will be human colonies on Mars as early as the year 2030.

____

2. I think that for native speakers of English, Spanish is a relatively easy language to learn.

____

3. Maybe the whale shark looks like a whale, but in fact it is a fish.

____

4. I think the Sixth Symphony is proof that Beethoven was, at heart, a romantic composer.

____

5. Maybe it will cost the city of Los Angeles more than $2 billion to fund its plan to create affordable housing for its homeless population.

____

6. Considering the recent shaky performance of the stock market, I think the U.S. Federal Reserve probably will not raise interest rates again this year.

____

7. Despite the academic advantages it offers, I think a year-round school calendar is not a practical alternative for the Glendale school system.

____

8. Some would say that maybe the personal computer was the most important invention of the late 20th century.

____

Academic Vocabulary

Modal + Verb Combinations Frequently Used in Academic Writing

can help	could lead	may need	might have	should be taken
cannot be	may be	may result	must be received	would have been

Source: Corpus of Contemporary American English (Davies 2008–)

ACTIVITY 7 Vocabulary in Academic Writing

Use the academic vocabulary to complete the sentences.

Subject Area	Example from Academic Writing
Education	**1.** Proof of a recent physical exam ________________ before students can attend public schools in most states.
Genetics	**2.** Research from the University of North Carolina suggests that genes rather than the home environment ________________ the reason why some children tend to resist trying new foods.
Psychology	**3.** Interestingly, some high-school graduates appeared unworried about their own adjustment to college and instead expressed concern that their parents ________________ a difficult time adjusting to their new status as "empty nesters."
Law	**4.** According to the Federal Rules of Evidence, a married person ________________ compelled to testify against his or her spouse in a court of law.
Ecology	**5.** In the next 50 years, habitat loss caused by human activity ________________ to the extinction of one-fourth of the world's plants and animals.
Health	**6.** Athletes, people who exercise a lot, and people who live in warm climates where they sweat a lot ________________ to supplement their food with extra salt in order to maintain the proper electrolyte balance in the blood.
Geology	**7.** During the first hours after an asteroid hit the earth 66 million years ago, scientists say there ________________ total darkness.
Medicine	**8.** Thyroid medication ________________ first thing in the morning on an empty stomach.
Botany	**9.** Mulch serves several purposes in a garden. It ________________ save water, prevent weeds, and protect fragile plants from both heat and cold.
Business	**10.** Economists predict that an increase in California's business tax rate ________________ in businesses relocating overseas or to states with a more favorable business climate.

Put It Together

ACTIVITY 8 Review Quiz

Multiple Choice Choose the letter of the correct answer.

1. It is estimated that by 2025, Tokyo ______ a population of roughly 40 million people.

   a. could to have **b.** must have **c.** will have **d.** maybe has

2. A shortage of trained pilots ______ cause some smaller airlines to cut flights and reduce service to smaller airports.

   a. should **b.** might be **c.** will maybe **d.** could soon

3. Some people say that the extensive flood damage following Hurricane Katrina in August 2005 ______ prevented if the flood walls had been double-checked.

   a. was supposed to be **b.** might have been **c.** might be **d.** was able to be

4. The World Health Organization recommends that healthy adults ______ eat less than 2,000 mg of sodium and at least 3,510 mg of potassium per day.

   a. should **b.** would **c.** will **d.** maybe

5. Various studies tried to show that ancient people ______ blue as a distinct color, separate from green.

   a. should not have seen **b.** did not have to see **c.** were not able to see **d.** will see

Error Correction One of the five underlined words or phrases is not correct. Find the error and correct it. Be prepared to explain your answer.

6. <u>Because of</u> their size, keen eyesight, and powerful kick, adult giraffes are not <u>usually attacked</u> by predators, but young giraffes <u>may to be killed</u> by lions <u>as well as</u> leopards and hyenas. Only one-fourth to one-half of baby giraffes <u>reach</u> adulthood.

7. A hypothetical essay <u>written</u> by G. M. Trevelyan in 1907 speculated <u>that</u> England <u>would have suffered</u> economically and many people <u>would have starve</u> if the Duke of Wellington <u>had not defeated</u> Napoleon at the Battle of Waterloo in 1815.

8. <u>In</u> 2014, physicists used a <u>scientific process</u> called carbon dating to <u>prove</u> that a famous painting, once <u>thought to be</u> the work of the French painter Ferdinand Leger, <u>could not has been</u> painted by him.

Chocolate is stirred in a huge vat for 72 hours.

ACTIVITY 9 Building Greater Sentences

Combine these short sentences into one sentence. You can add new words and move words around, but you should not add or omit any ideas. More than one answer is possible, but these sentences require modals.

1. **a.** Dark chocolate contains chemical compounds.
   b. They are called flavonoids.
   c. They may have the potential to fight off diseases.
   d. The diseases include diabetes, stroke, cancer, and heart disease.

2. **a.** This happened in 1926.
   b. The inventor Nikola Tesla predicted something.
   c. He wrote that women could "surpass men in every field."

3. **a.** A 29-mile (46.7 km) bridge could be built.
   b. It will span the Red Sea between Yemen and Djibouti.
   c. It will connect the continents of Asia and Africa.
   d. It could be built by the year 2020.

ACTIVITY 10 Steps to Composing

Read the essay. Then follow the directions in the 10 steps to edit the information and composition of the essay. Write your revised essay on a separate sheet of paper. Be careful with capitalization and punctuation. Check your answers with the class.

ADVANTAGES–DISADVANTAGES ESSAY

Driverless Cars

[1] The development of autonomous driving systems—driverless cars—has advanced rapidly since Google introduced the first driverless vehicle in 2012. [2] Several U.S. states have passed laws allowing driverless cars. [3] Some experts predict that driverless cars will be in wide use all over the world by the year 2020.

[4] Driverless cars would offer some important advantages, according to their supporters. [5] First is the reduced risk of crashes. [6] The vehicles are operated by computers instead of error-prone human drivers. [7] Second is better traffic flow thanks to coordination between vehicles. [8] This eliminates the need for traffic signals. [9] Third, and possibly most significant, is the ability of passengers to use travel time in any way they choose.

[10] But new research from the University of Leeds warns that driverless cars will change our relationship with our cars and will possibly reduce or eliminate these benefits. [11] Lead author Dr. Zia Wadud explains that driverless cars will cause an actual increase in car use because people who want to use their commute time efficiently will use driverless cars instead of public transportation. [12] In the worst case, this change will increase road use by as much as 60 percent. [13] This is according to the Leeds study. [14] Moreover, possible higher speed limits because of the improved safety of driverless cars will reduce energy efficiency.

[15] The Leeds researchers conclude that driverless technology will have both pros and cons. [16] In the end, they say, governments will need to determine the best way to manage these impacts.

1. It is not good to repeat the same word or phrase too often. In sentences 2, 4, 10, and 11, replace *driverless cars* with other phrases. Choose among *driverless vehicles, driverless technology, autonomous vehicles, autonomous driving systems,* and *autonomous cars.*
2. Combine sentences 2 and 3.
3. Combine sentences 5 and 6 with *since.*
4. Combine sentences 7 and 8 by changing sentence 8 to a phrase beginning with *eliminating.*
5. It is usually not good to start a sentence with a conjunction. Replace *But* in sentence 10 with a transition.
6. Good academic writers use hedging to reduce the risk of error. Replace *will* with *may, might,* or *could* in sentences 3, 10 (twice), 11 (twice), and 12.
7. Eliminate *This is* in sentence 13 and combine sentences 12 and 13.
8. In sentence 14, change *will* to a "softer" modal to make the statement less assertive.
9. Insert an adverb in sentence 15 to boost the force of the conclusion.
10. Add *probably* in sentence 16.

ACTIVITY 11 Original Writing

On a separate sheet of paper, write a summary (at least seven sentences) of a research study or a body of information from one of your academic courses. Discuss cause and effect or advantages and disadvantages. Use at least one example of a simple modal, past modal, or phrase for hedging and underline them; try to use two if possible.

Here are some examples of how to begin.

- *Samsung predicts that as technology progresses, we will probably be able to use 3-D printers to manufacture large structures like homes from recyclable materials.*
- *Experience in other countries suggests that lowering the voting age to 16 in the United States could motivate young people to become more engaged in the political process.*
- *The derailment of an Amtrak train on May 12, 2015, might not have occurred if several safety measures had been followed.*

An antenna serviceman works high atop the John Hancock Center in Chicago, Illinois.

7 Using Gerunds and Infinitives

WHAT DO YOU KNOW?

DISCUSS Look at the photo and read the caption. Discuss the questions.

1. How do you think this man feels about working so high above the ground? What do you think he likes about his job?
2. Can you name something that you are afraid of doing?

FIND THE ERRORS This paragraph contains one error with a gerund and one with an infinitive. Find the errors and correct them. Explain your corrections to a partner.

DESCRIPTIVE PARAGRAPH

Phobias

[1] A phobia is an anxiety disorder in which someone has a very strong but irrational fear of something. [2] Usually that fear is of something that presents very little or no threat to the person. [3] For example, claustrophobia is the fear of confined spaces, and acrophobia is the fear of heights. [4] There are some lesser-known phobias, too. [5] A person with agyrophobia has a fear of crossing streets, and a person with athazagoraphobia has a fear of be forgotten or ignored. [6] Although some people advise those with phobias avoiding what they are afraid of, this is not always realistic. [7] For example, a person with autophobia fears being alone and always needs to be around other people. [8] Fortunately, treatments do exist. [9] Treatment can come in the form of medicine, therapy, or a combination of the two. [10] Treatment can help with the symptoms most people with phobias share: a rapid heart rate, chest pain, trouble breathing, sweating, and trembling. [11] In many cases, treatment has been proven to help phobia sufferers.

Grammar Forms

7.1 Gerunds

A gerund is the base form of the verb + *-ing*. It acts as a noun and can be in the subject or object position in a sentence.

Position	Example
1. as the subject of a sentence	**Meditating** can help people who have a phobia.
2. as the object of certain verbs	Doctors sometimes suggest **meditating**.
3. as the object of a preposition	The point of **meditating** is to relax the mind and body.

Note

For the negative, use *not* + gerund.

They will regret **not participating** in the negotiations.

7.2 Infinitives

An infinitive is *to* + the base form of the verb. It is used:

Position	Example
1. after certain verbs	The company's marketing strategy failed **to attract** new customers.
2. after the construction of *it* + *be* + adjective	It is possible **to receive** on-the-job training for some careers.

Notes

1. For the negative, use *not* + infinitive.

   It is important **not to ignore** foreign market trends.
2. Although an infinitive can be used as a subject, it is more common to use a gerund as a subject in academic writing.

7.3 Common Verbs Followed by Gerunds and Infinitives

There is no easy way to determine if a verb should be followed by an infinitive or gerund. Study the patterns of these common verbs.

1. verb + gerund *appreciate, avoid, consider, delay, detest, discuss, dislike, enjoy, finish, involve, miss, postpone, practice, recommend, risk, suggest*	Nutritionists often **recommend including** supplemental vitamins as a part of a daily regimen.

7.3	Common Verbs Followed by Gerunds and Infinitives (Continued)
2. verb + infinitive *afford, agree, ask, decide, demand, deserve, expect, hesitate, hope, intend, learn, need, offer, plan, pretend, promise, refuse, seem, tend, volunteer, wait, want, wish*	The average person's diet **needs to include** 13 vitamins: A, C, D, E, K, and all the B vitamins, such as thiamine and riboflavin.
3. verb + gerund *or* verb + infinitive *attempt, begin, continue, hate, like, love, prefer, start, stop, quit*	Many individuals **prefer getting** their nutrition from food rather than supplements. Many individuals **prefer to get** their nutrition from food rather than supplements.

Note

Verbs that can be followed by either a gerund or an infinitive often have little change in meaning. For some verbs, however, the meaning is completely different, for example: *stop, forget, remember.*

The team **stopped to assess** the situation. = *The team stopped doing something and is now assessing the situation.*

The team **stopped assessing** the situation. = *The team is no longer assessing the situation.*

ACTIVITY 1

For each sentence, underline the correct word in parentheses.

1. Some politicians want (*reducing* / *to reduce*) CO_2 emissions in an effort to save the earth.
2. Sociologists state that it is often finances that help a mother decide (*working* / *to work*) outside the home.
3. The two most well-known scholars in this field suggest (*adding* / *to add*) four new elements to the periodic table.
4. Medical students practice (*preparing* / *to prepare*) for surgery by operating on lifelike mannequins rather than real people.
5. With a failing economy, economists expect (*seeing* / *to see*) credit card debt rising and online shopping falling.
6. This research discusses (*using* / *to use*) four models to determine the validity of the results.
7. Most actors hope (*not being* / *not to be*) cast in the same types of roles again and again.
8. Clinicians would like (*looking* / *to look*) at scientific research about the Ebola virus to improve procedures that prevent and treat the disease.

ACTIVITY 2

Write the gerund or infinitive form of the verb in parentheses. In some cases, both forms may be correct.

1. Critics strongly recommend ______________________ (*study*) *Othello* by William Shakespeare because of its tragic hero and other interesting characters.
2. The presidential candidates agreed ______________________ (*not, focus*) on personal attacks.
3. For decades psychologists have continued ______________________ (*debate*) the importance of nature versus nurture.
4. The respondent indicated that she forgot ______________________ (*write*) the note. She was unable to recall the note she wrote. Researchers noted that the medication may cause memory loss.
5. In order to become president of the United States, a person needs ______________________ (*be*) 35 years old, born in the country, and to have lived in the country for 14 years.
6. The journalists decided ______________________ (*not, discuss*) the sensitive information.
7. As expected, the group stopped ______________________ (*work*) when they heard the alarm sound.
8. When the time is right, the leader will stop ______________________ (*ask*) if all trainees understand. This will help assure that no one falls behind.
9. In order to avoid ______________________ (*create*) additional delays, the budget was quickly approved.
10. People around the world like ______________________ (*celebrate*) New Year's Eve on December 31 since it is the last day of of the Gregorian calendar.

Common Uses

7.4 Using Gerunds and Infinitives as Nouns

Gerunds and infinitives function as nouns and noun phrases.

1. A gerund is often used as a subject of a sentence or a clause. An infinitive can also be a subject, but this is less common.	When you are a parent, **quitting** is not an option. The patient did not realize that **eating** was prohibited after midnight.
2. Gerunds are used as objects of a preposition.	Health experts say that a benefit of **running** is an improved mood.
3. Gerunds and infinitives are used as objects of certain verbs. (See chart 7.3.)	Residents should **avoid taking** the highway during a storm, as flooding may occur. Many businesses **decided to donate** household supplies to the tsunami victims.

Notes

1. Gerund subjects are singular and take a singular verb. However, there are some cases where a compound gerund subject requires a plural verb.

   Reviewing the lab results is an important step.

   Reviewing the results and developing a report **are** the next steps.

2. Be careful to use a gerund when *to* is a preposition. Common verb + *to* combinations include: *be used to, be accustomed to, look forward to,* and *be opposed to.*

   The man <u>was not accustomed to</u> **being** questioned by his employees.

3. Use the preposition *by* + gerund to explain how something happens or happened.

   Students wrote their own paragraph **by following** a model.

7.5 Other Uses of Infinitives

Some other uses of infinitives are common in academic writing.

1. Infinitives are often used as a reduction of *in order to* to show purpose.	
a. Often, the infinitive is preferred in academic papers to cut down on wordiness.	**In order to complete** the experiment, the team needed to redo one of the tests.
b. Use *in order to* if the writing is very formal, for example, a letter to someone important.	**To complete** the experiment, the team needed to redo one of the tests. I would like meet with you **in order to** learn about the culture at your company.
c. Use *in order to* with negative infinitives.	**In order not to raise** suspicion, the congressman left the dinner.

7.5	Other Uses of Infinitives (Continued)
2. When the verb is *be*, the subject complement is often an infinitive.	The company's goal is **to determine** the best path forward given its financial situation.
3. Use an infinitive after phrases beginning with *it* + *be* + adjective. Some common adjectives include: *challenging, difficult, exciting, good, hard, important, impossible, likely, smart, wise.*	Doctors and researchers agree that it is important **to get** at least seven hours of sleep per night.

ACTIVITY 3

Underline the correct answer in parentheses.

1. (*Starting / To start*) a new business can be extremely challenging.
2. Most analysts agree that it is impossible (*getting / to get*) gun laws changed in the United States.
3. Virologists are interested in (*studying / to study*) how the human body fights diseases.
4. (*Running / To run*) a fever of greater than 108 degrees Fahrenheit (42°C) is extremely dangerous and can even lead to death.
5. (*Writing / To write*) an excellent research paper, students should start with a strong research question.
6. The cost of (*advertising / to advertise*) on national TV is extremely expensive.
7. A great many educators believe that (*being / to be*) able to read at an early age is a huge advantage for later learning.
8. (*Learning / To learn*) a foreign language well, it is important to practice in realistic situations.
9. Over the next 20 years, climatologists expect ______________ (*seeing / to see*) rising average temperatures.
10. The psychology study involved ______________ (*testing / to test*) three different groups of participants.

ACTIVITY 4

In each set of sentences, fill in the blank with the gerund or infinitive form of the verb in parentheses.

1. According to the Southern California Earthquake Center, people need ______________ (*prepare*) a disaster kit before an earthquake strikes. A dust mask, good shoes, and cash are items people might not consider ______________ (*add*), but they are recommended.

2. ______________ (*study*) math and science is not as popular as studying business. As a result, the U.S. federal government intends ______________ (*invest*) millions of dollars in programs that promote science, technology, engineering, and math. ______________ (*emphasize*) these topics might encourage students to major in these fields in college and enter promising careers.

3. According to the company's Web site, ______________ (*work*) out with a personal trainer can increase a person's motivation and lead to better physical results. ______________ (*postpone*) the decision to hire a trainer usually postpones the actual physical exercise. Therefore, it is best ______________ (*hire*) a trainer as soon as possible in order to begin a regular exercise routine.

4. Photosynthesis is a process that plants use ______________ (*convert*) light energy into chemical energy. ______________ (*release*) the chemical energy allows plants to grow.

5. ______________ (*run*) races was one of the first athletic events in the Olympic Games. It was in the 18th Olympiad that ______________ (*wrestle*) was added. In today's Olympics, there are many more athletic events included.

6. Art students often want ______________ (*focus*) on one type of art, such as painting or sculpture. However, they need ______________ (*study*) the general features all art shares, such as design and style.

7. In China, mooncakes are a popular food ______________ (*eat*) during the Mid-Autumn Festival.

8. ______________ (*have*) only two runways has not kept Dubai International Airport from ______________ (*be*) one of the world's busiest airports. In 2015, the airport handled over 75 million passengers, 2.5 million tons of cargo, and 400,000 aircraft.

Common Errors

Common Error 7.1 Do you need a gerund as the subject?

Reading
~~To read~~ a text that explains Sigmund Freud's definitions of the id, ego, and superego is essential for any solid psychology research.

REMEMBER: A gerund is more commonly used as a subject than an infinitive.

Common Error 7.2 Does the verb agree with the gerund subject?

is
Exercising every day for 30 minutes ~~are~~ strongly recommended by the American Heart Association to improve cardiovascular health.

are
Exercising moderately and eating a well-balanced diet ~~is~~ recommended by the American Heart Association.

REMEMBER:
- Do not use a plural verb form with a gerund when it is the subject of the sentence. Even if the object after the gerund is plural, the verb should be singular.
- If the subject consists of two or more gerunds, the verb is plural.

ACTIVITY 5 **Common Errors 7.1 and 7.2**

Underline the gerund subjects. Then underline the correct form of the verb *be*.

1. Supporting public service and the space program (*was / were*) important to President John F. Kennedy.
2. Reporting results and interpreting data (*is / are*) necessary to succeed in academic studies at the college level.
3. Including strong characters, an interesting plot, and a moral lesson (*was / were*) what made Chaucer one of the best writers of medieval times.
4. Reading *Eugene Onegin* by Pushkin and *War and Peace* by Tolstoy (*is / are*) a good introduction to Russian literature.
5. Applying mathematics and examining empirical evidence (*is / are*) two things that most engineering fields share.
6. Being creative and managing emotions (*is / are*) functions of the right side of the brain.

7. Driving cars or trucks (*is / are*) a basic job requirement for certain entry-level positions.

8. Online shopping by consumers (*has been / have been*) growing in popularity; last year millions of dollars were spent at amazon.com alone.

9. Managing time and studying effectively (*is / are*) skills college students must learn in order to earn good grades during their first year.

10. Evaluating and studying behavior (*is / are*) things psychologists typically do during a session with a patient.

Common Error 7.3 Is *to* a preposition or part of an infinitive?

Some people object to ~~use~~ using stem cells for research because there is a risk that the cells might cause cancer.

REMEMBER: Sometimes *to* is a preposition, not part of an infinitive. Use *to* + gerund when *to* is a preposition.

Common Error 7.4 Do you have *by* + gerund?

By ~~sign~~ signing the Treaty of Versailles, the Allied powers brought World War I to an end.

REMEMBER: Use *by* + gerund to explain how something happens at a point in time.

ACTIVITY 6 Common Errors 7.3 and 7.4

Each of the following sentences contains an error. Underline and correct the error.

1. By study the brains of American football players, Dr. Bennet Ifeakandu Omalu was the first to discover chronic traumatic encephalopathy (CTE) in professional athletes.

2. Some educators are opposed to give standardized tests because the tests cover material not taught in classrooms.

3. During a year of heavy rain, farmers look forward to see higher yields in wheat crops.

4. F. Scott Fitzgerald continued his education after graduating from the Newman School by attend Princeton University.

5. The explorers were used to see snakes and other wildlife after living in the jungle for a few months.

6. By insist, actress Natalie Portman was able to have a female director in the movie about Supreme Court Justice Ruth Bader Ginsburg.

7. Many students are kinesthetic learners, meaning that they learn something by do it.

8. The skier hoped to survive a possible avalanche by use her new safety device, an air bag that inflates in seconds after pulling a cord.

Climbers watch an avalanche happening in Denali National Park and Preserve, Alaska.

Academic Vocabulary

Gerunds and Infinitives Frequently Used in Academic Writing

Gerunds		Infinitives	
becoming	making	to be	to make
being	using	to do	to use
having		to have	

Source: Corpus of Contemporary American English (Davies 2008)

ACTIVITY 7 Vocabulary in Academic Writing

Use the academic vocabulary words in the infinitive or gerund form to complete the sentences.

Subject Area	Example from Academic Writing
Education	**1.** Understanding what students need ____________ successful has given new insights to the administrators of the program.
Nursing	**2.** Doctors cannot avoid ____________ aware of a patient's allergies when prescribing medicine to treat other conditions.
Political Science	**3.** The president avoided ____________ a promise that his social services program would benefit the poorest citizens in the country.
Psychology	**4.** Everyone copes with death differently. For example, some people refuse to read any materials that have ____________ with dying; others feel more in control if they know more so they read everything they can.
English Composition	**5.** Many people avoided ____________ fast food after watching the documentary *Super Size Me* because the movie convinced people that they needed to be more aware of what they were eating.
Medical	**6.** After studying the samples, approximately one-half were found ____________ abnormalities.
Sociology	**7.** To avoid ____________ a victim of identity theft, do not share personal information with individuals or companies that you do not trust.
Business	**8.** Being prepared ____________ a variety of social media and electronic communication tools has helped companies propel sales to the next level.
Economics	**9.** To make predictions about the future, economists avoid ____________ rumors as a basis for their predictions and pay attention to figures compiled from the current state of the stock market.
Art	**10.** Many artists now use trash ____________ a piece of art. For example, some artists are using electronic trash to create sculptures.

Put It Together

ACTIVITY 8 Review Quiz

Multiple Choice Choose the letter of the correct answer.

1. Extensive changes need _____ if we want to reverse the tremendous amount of damage that has already been done to the environment.

   a. to happen **b.** happen **c.** happening **d.** happens

2. Because of the reaction of the combined chemicals, the scientists considered _____ the ratio of the ingredients.

   a. to change **b.** a change **c.** changing **d.** change

3. Not _____ enough sleep is harmful to a person's well-being because it adversely affects both the physical and mental states.

   a. to get **b.** get **c.** getting **d.** gets

4. Often government officials intend _____ the best they can for the citizens, but sometimes the results do not seem that way.

   a. have done **b.** do **c.** doing **d.** to do

5. There is no reason to be afraid of _____ a medical degree despite the fact that the science courses can be challenging.

   a. to pursue **b.** pursuing **c.** pursue **d.** the pursuit

Error Correction One of the five underlined words or phrases is not correct. Find the error and correct it. Be prepared to explain your answer.

6. Researchers suggest to do more research on the long-term effects that chemotherapy has on a person's brain, such as thinking, remembering, and processing.

7. Building the best possible database, the company spent millions on software programs, new computers, and employee training. Using the database is easy after employees learn to manage three basic procedures.

8. College students are responsible for maintain good grades and attending all classes. They must also be good at managing their time and be ready to choose a major in their sophomore year.

A doctor monitors results as an athlete wearing an oxygen mask runs on a treadmill.

ACTIVITY 9 Building Greater Sentences

Combine these short sentences into one sentence. You can add new words and move words around, but you should not add or omit any ideas. More than one answer is possible, but these sentences require gerunds or infinitives.

1. **a.** Doctors recommend running on a treadmill.
   b. Running on a treadmill will help patients lose weight.
   c. Patients need a healthy heart to run on a treadmill.

2. **a.** A marketing team changed its focus from television commercials.
   b. It allocated its funding to social media.
   c. The team wanted to target young people.
   d. Young people are going online more than they are watching television.

3. **a.** Selecting new classes each semester is difficult.
   b. Buying the correct textbooks for new classes each semester is difficult.
   c. Some students are good at completing these two tasks.
   d. These tasks are important.

ACTIVITY 10 Steps to Composing

Read the paragraph. Then follow the directions in the 10 steps to edit the information and composition of the paragraph. Write your revised paragraph on a separate piece of paper. Be careful with capitalization and punctuation. Check your answers with the class.

CAUSE–EFFECT PARAGRAPH

Treating Acne

[1] Dermatologists hope to find a cure for acne, which is a problem for many adolescents. [2] In the past, teenagers were told that not eating chocolate or junk food would help. [3] Today, some acne can be treated with topical creams. [4] The creams unblock clogged pores. [5] Sometimes these creams are combined with an antibiotic, such as doxycycline. [6] Doctors must be careful. [7] Antibiotics have side effects. [8] For example, doxycycline causes sensitivity to the sun. [9] Tetracycline makes teeth turn yellow. [10] Sometimes acne can be aggravated by other things, such as cosmetics. [11] Dermatologists may ask patients to stop using makeup. [12] Sometimes when a person stops the use of makeup, the acne goes away on its own and no medical treatment is needed. [13] Doctors are currently conducting a tremendous amount of research on this problem.

1. In the first sentence, add the adjective *common.*
2. In sentence 2, change *that not* to *to avoid* to give a more academic tone. Make any other necessary changes.
3. Connect sentences 3 and 4; combine the sentence with the word *that* and delete *the creams* to avoid using the same noun twice.
4. In sentence 5, add *or tetracycline, which is a second antibiotic.*
5. Combine sentences 6 and 7 to avoid two short, choppy sentences.
6. In sentence 8, add the modal *can* and make any other necessary changes.
7. In sentence 9, change the word *make* to the verb *cause* because *make* is a weak verb and *cause* is more accurate. Make any other necessary changes.
8. In sentence 10, add the gerund *wearing* before *cosmetics.*

9. In sentence 12, add a gerund in place of *the use*. Make any other necessary changes.

10. Begin the last sentence with the infinitive of purpose: *To help people who suffer from acne*. Be sure to add appropriate punctuation.

ACTIVITY 11 Original Writing

On a separate sheet of paper, write a cause–effect paragraph (at least seven sentences) about a great achievement. Include why this achievement was important and what the person did to achieve it. Use at least one gerund and one infinitive; underline them. Try to use more if possible.

Here are some examples of how to begin.

- *By ending slavery, Abraham Lincoln changed the course of U.S. history.*
- *Dustin Moskovitz is one of the world's youngest billionaires. He became rich after cofounding Facebook.*
- *Edward Jenner developed the first successful vaccine for smallpox. Developing this vaccine led to eradication of the disease in the 20th century.*

A student at the University of Wisconsin is wired with sensors as part of a sleep deprivation study.

8 Using the Passive Voice

WHAT DO YOU KNOW?

DISCUSS Look at the photo and read the caption. Discuss the questions.

1. What kinds of information can be collected from the brain sensors?
2. Would you want to participate in this kind of study? Why or why not?

FIND THE ERRORS This paragraph contains two errors with the passive voice. Find the errors and correct them. Explain your corrections to a partner.

SUMMARY PARAGRAPH

Our Brains Are Designed to Do Good

[1] In a study that was published in 2016, scientists determined that our brains influence altruism. [2] When people are altruistic, they are generous to others, even at a cost to themselves. [3] In the first part of the study, participants shown a video of someone being poked with a pin. [4] Then they were shown photos of faces with a variety of emotions and were asked to imitate the expressions on the faces. [5] Their brains were scanned to see what areas were active when they felt pain or empathy, or when they were imitating others. [6] Next, the participants played a game. [7] In the game they were given $10 and they had to decide how much to award to a stranger. [8] Those with the most activity in the areas of the brain associated with empathy and imitating others were given 75 percent of their money to the stranger.

Grammar Forms

8.1 Passive Voice

In the passive voice, the subject receives the action of the verb. To form the passive voice, use a form of *be* + the past participle of the verb.

Active voice: Airports **implemented** new airport security measures.

Passive voice: New airport security measures **were implemented**.

	Form	Example
Simple Present	*am / is / are* (+ *not*) + past participle	A new approach **is needed** in the war on poverty.
Simple Past	*was / were* (+ *not*) + past participle	The side effects of thalidomide **were not known** in the 1960s.
Present Perfect	*has / have* (+ *not*) + *been* + past participle	Fairy circles, which are mysterious patterns on dry earth, **have been found** in Africa and now, in Australia.
Modals	*modal* (+ *not*) + *be* + past participle	Cardiovascular disease later in life **may be related** to eating behaviors in young children.
Modals of Past Possibility	*modal* (+ *not*) + *have* + *been* + past participle	Much of the damage **could have been prevented** if certain procedures had been in place.
Gerund	(*not* +) *being* + past participle	The sense of **being treated** unfairly at work can cause depression.
Infinitive	(*not* +) *to be* + past participle	Safety concerns regarding nuclear power plants need **to be addressed**.

Notes

1. Do not use passive voice with intransitive verbs (verbs that cannot take an object).
   Nelson Mandela died a few years ago. (Not: ~~A few years ago was died Nelson Mandela.~~)
2. Passive voice occurs most commonly in simple present and simple past, followed by present perfect and modals. It is very rare in progressive forms.
3. Sometimes *by* + the agent (or *doer* of the action) comes at the end of a passive sentence.
   Active: **Zaha Hadid** designed the new maritime terminal in Salerno, Italy.
   Passive: The new maritime terminal in Salerno, Italy, was designed **by Zaha Hadid**.
4. Modals of past possibility include *could, should, would, might, must* + *have been* + past participle.

ACTIVITY 1

Fill in the blank with the passive form of the verb in parentheses.

1. Antioxidants, although generally healthy, ______________________ (*find,* present perfect) to fuel some cancer cells.
2. Friends ______________________ (*classify,* modal *can*) by how close you feel to them: acquaintances, casual friends, or confidants.
3. Driverless cars ______________________ (*design,* simple present) to operate automatically and may therefore reduce driver error and fuel consumption.
4. Researchers discourage the routine prescription of antibiotics for colds, as this practice ______________________ (*know,* simple present) to contribute to the development of superbugs, or resistant bacteria.
5. The mandatory sentencing laws passed in the 1990s ______________________ (*intend,* simple past) to eliminate unfairness in sentencing, but they resulted in keeping people in prison for many years for relatively minor crimes.
6. The range of responses to the questionnaire ______________________ (*present,* simple present) in table 1.4.
7. Some people are embarrassed about ______________________ (*treat,* gerund) for mental illness and this may keep them from getting the help they need.
8. Historians have debated whether the American Civil War ______________________ (*avoid,* past modal *could*), but many believe the issue of slavery was too divisive.
9. The results of the survey still need ______________________ (*analyze,* infinitive).
10. New techniques ______________________ (*develop,* present perfect) that help prevent an allergic response to peanuts.

Common Uses

8.2 Using the Passive

The passive voice is used more commonly in academic writing than in more informal writing. While sentences in active voice are often considered stronger and clearer, passive voice is commonly used:

1. to focus attention on new or important ideas or information by placing it at the beginning of the sentence	Barack Obama **was** first **elected** president in 2008.
a. Moving the object to the subject position can provide cohesion between ideas or paragraphs	The art world has long admired Banksy, a mysterious street artist. In spite of great efforts, Banksy's identity **has not been confirmed**.
b. Use a *by*-phrase when it is important to know who the agent is	The *Mona Lisa* **was painted** by Leonardo da Vinci in the early 16th century.
2. to avoid repetitive or unnecessary information about the agent of the action	Students **were tested** at the beginning and end of the semester. (We assume teachers were the agents, or the ones who tested the students.) Male professors are much more likely **to be described** as "brilliant" in student evaluations. (We know students describe the professors because these are "student evaluations.")
3. to express information in a more polite way or to avoid blaming someone; a *by* phrase is not used in this context	The candidate **was accused** of spreading false rumors about his competition. Students **are not** always **given** the option of retaking a test. He apologized for remarks that **were considered** offensive.
4. to convey objectivity and an impersonal tone • This is common in scientific papers, especially the methods and materials section of a scientific report. • About 30 percent of clauses in scientific articles are passive.	Participants **should be given** as much information as possible about the research ahead of time. Results **were analyzed** with a standard statistical method.

Notes
1. Passive voice is also a way to avoid using personal pronouns such as *I* and *we* as they are often discouraged in academic writing. Likewise, impersonal pronouns such as *someone* are vague and can weaken a sentence.
2. Adverbs can be used to modify a passive verb. In the simple present and past, they appear between *be* and the past participle. With perfect tenses or modals, they appear after the modal or form of *have* and before *be*.

   Negative campaign ads **are** often **used** in presidential elections.

   The ad **will not** likely **be aired** again as it was considered offensive and untrue.

ACTIVITY 2

Read each set of sentences. Underline the correct form of the words in parentheses.

1. A link (*has found / has been found*) between activity in a particular structure of the brain and creative problem-solving. According to researchers at Stanford University, activity in the cerebellum (*involves / is involved*) in the creative process, whereas greater activity in the parts of the brain that help you plan and manage (*impairs / is impaired*) creativity.

2. Exports (*fell / were fallen*) dramatically in the last quarter. Some of the decline in exports (*could attribute / could be attributed*) to the holidays and bad weather, but not all. Analysts (*expected / were expected*) exports to increase and (*surprised / were surprised*) by the numbers.

3. After Austria-Hungary (*defeated / was defeated*) in World War I, a new country (*created / was created*) that (*included / was included*) Serbia, Bosnia, Croatia, Montenegro, and Herzegovina. This new country of Yugoslavia (*dissolved / was dissolved*) during World War II and the rise of the Axis powers. The second Yugoslavia (*formed / was formed*) in 1946, and it (*covered / was covered*) the earlier territory as well as some land acquired from Italy. Economic problems (*led / were led*) to the breakup of Yugoslavia in the 1990s.

4. Over the last few years, food companies (*have mixed / have been mixed*) fruits and vegetables into other products. For example, spinach (*has added / has been added*) to pasta, and applesauce has been added to brownies. These tricks (*have tried / have been tried*) by desperate parents for a long time in their quest to get picky children to eat more healthy foods. However, some health experts (*bother / are bothered*) by this new trend. They (*fear / are feared*) that children (*will not learn / will not be learned*) healthy eating habits this way.

Common Errors

Common Error 8.1 Do you use the correct form of the verb?

Several languages are ~~spoke~~ spoken in Switzerland.

REMEMBER: Use the past participle after *be* in passive voice.

ACTIVITY 3 Common Error 8.1

Fill in the blank with the correct form of the verb in parentheses.

1. The study was ____________ (*conduct*) by researchers in several countries.
2. The results can be ____________ (*see*) in table 3.2.
3. Crows are ____________ (*know*) to be curious and intelligent.
4. Many sports figures have been ____________ (*accuse*) of using drugs or other banned substances.
5. Even being ____________ (*consider*) for the award is a great honor.
6. Matisse may have been ____________ (*influence*) by an exhibit of African sculptures at Trocodero Museum before he decided to travel to North Africa in 1906.
7. More money was ____________ (*spend*) to host the Sochi Winter Olympics in Russia than to host any other Olympic Games.
8. According to Malcolm Gladwell in his book *Blink*, judgments that are ____________ (*make*) within just a few seconds are often remarkably accurate.

Common Error 8.2 Do you include a form of *be* in the passive voice?

Mo Yan ^was interviewed after winning the Nobel Prize for Literature in 2012.

REMEMBER: You must use a form of *be* with the past participle in passive voice.

ACTIVITY 4 Common Error 8.2

Read the sentences. Find where the *be* forms are missing. Write a correction above where the missing word(s) should be. Some sentences have more than one missing form of *be*.

1. Seed banks usually designed to protect biodiversity by storing seeds in climate-controlled vaults.
2. Because lying often accompanied by feelings of guilt, it creates stress which can detected by lie detector machines.
3. Recently, certain disease-resistant crops have developed through genetic modification, but some consumers refuse to eat them.
4. Risk factors for heart disease that have identified include obesity, smoking, diabetes, and high cholesterol.
5. The Greek philosopher Aristotle known as the father of political science.
6. In the report released a few years ago, investigators determined that efforts made to cover up the disaster.
7. Bananas picked while they are still green and then shipped around the world.
8. Although it painted several hundred years ago, the *Mona Lisa* still considered a great work of art, though this may be due more to its fame than to its actual artistic qualities.

Crowds of visitors take photos of the *Mona Lisa* at the Louvre Museum in Paris, France.

Common Error 8.3 Do you need passive or active voice?

Perhaps as many as 100 million people ~~were died~~ died as a result of the 1918 influenza pandemic.

REMEMBER: Use passive voice only with transitive verbs when the subject of the sentence receives the action.

ACTIVITY 5 Common Error 8.3

Underline the correct form of the verb in parentheses.

1. British researchers recently (*tested / were tested*) the effect that the time of a vaccination (*had / was had*) on effectiveness. They (*found / were found*) that people who (*give / are given*) a flu vaccine in the morning (*protect better / are better protected*) than those who (*vaccinate / are vaccinated*) in the afternoon.

2. Research (*has shown / has been shown*) that walking in parks and other green spaces (*reduces / is reduced*) stress. In a new study, researchers (*wanted / were wanted*) to find out if photos of green spaces (*could do / could be done*) the same thing. Sensors that monitor heart activity (*attached / were attached*) to participants. Then the participants (*gave / were given*) a stressful test. Afterward, they (*showed / were shown*) either photos of trees or of buildings. Those who (*saw / were seen*) trees (*had / were had*) lower heart rates.

3. Workers in their forties often (*experience / are experienced*) dissatisfaction with their jobs. This dissatisfaction (*often causes / is often caused*) by a feeling that earlier expectations (*have not met / have not been met*). For example, if you (*thought / were thought*) you would be head of a company and you are not, you might (*feel / be felt*) like a failure. Highly dissatisfied employees are more likely (*to report / to be reported*) stress and physical pain, and are more likely (*to diagnose / to be diagnosed*) with depression.

Academic Vocabulary

Passive Verb Forms Frequently Used in Academic Writing

can be seen	has been made	is known	was based	were asked
can be used	have been found	is needed	was conducted	was reported

Source: Corpus of Contemporary American English (Davies 2008–)

ACTIVITY 6 Vocabulary in Academic Writing

Use the academic vocabulary words in the passive forms given above to complete the sentences.

Subject Area	Example from Academic Writing
Education	**1.** A study ______________________ to determine if *gamification*, or adding games to classroom tasks, could improve math scores, and it found that scores improved 17 percent on a statewide assessment.
Environmental Science	**2.** The decline in Arctic sea ice ______________________ in figure 3, which compares ice extent in 1979 with that in 2014.
English Composition	**3.** When a decision ______________________ on your application, a letter is sent informing you of the outcome.
Business	**4.** When consumers ______________________ what *natural* on a label for packaged food means, most thought it meant that the food did not contain artificial ingredients or colors.
Psychology	**5.** An MRI ______________________ to show functional activity in the brain, which means that researchers can see which parts of the brain are working on particular tasks.
Health	**6.** Many toxins contribute to a greater risk for cancer, including arsenic in drinking water, which ______________________ to cause skin cancer.
Film Studies	**7.** The movie *The Social Network* ______________________ on Mark Zuckerberg and the creation of Facebook.
Economics	**8.** Although fracking provides jobs and lowers fuel costs, further research ______________________ to determine whether the economic benefits outweigh the environmental costs.
Archaeology	**9.** Fossils from more than 6,000 early humans ______________________, allowing scientists to understand more about how people have adapted over time.
Sociology	**10.** According to a report on cyberbullying between 2004 and 2010, only one in five cases ______________________ to authorities.

ACTIVITY 7 Review Quiz

Multiple Choice Choose the letter of the correct answer.

1. Peace talks ______ after the attacks last week.

   a. suspend **b.** were suspended **c.** suspended **d.** can be suspended

2. Students ______ to register before the start of each semester.

   a. are required **b.** require **c.** has been required **d.** required

3. Elephants ______ not only grieving for their own dead, but grieving for the dead of other species.

   a. were observing **b.** observed **c.** have observed **d.** have been observed

4. Tennis ______ on different surfaces, including clay and grass.

   a. played **b.** plays **c.** is play **d.** can be played

5. Sun Tzu's *The Art of War* ______ in China in the 5th century BCE.

   a. was written **b.** wrote **c.** can be written **d.** was writing

Error Correction One of the five underlined words or phrases is not correct. Find the error and correct it. Be prepared to explain your answer.

6. In a recent study, researchers have found that students' test performance can be improve if children are put to bed at the same time every night.

7. Applicants who hope to considered for the interior design program should read the information packet carefully, as the program requires students to complete many time-consuming projects.

8. The World Health Organization has released a report about weather that is caused by the climate pattern known as El Niño, which has been created major disruptions around the world, including droughts in India and floods in Paraguay.

Dark blue tiger butterflies are common all over Malaysia.

ACTIVITY 8 Building Greater Sentences

Combine these short sentences into one sentence. You can add new words and move words around, but you should not add or omit any ideas. More than one answer is possible, but all of these sentences require the passive voice.

1. **a.** People find more than 1,000 species of butterflies in Peninsular Malaysia.
   b. There was a recent study of butterflies.
   c. The study was in the parks of Kuala Lumpur.
   d. They recorded only 60 species of butterflies in the parks.

   ____

   ____

2. **a.** Someone developed a new system.
   b. It allows Web users to share aspects of their online activity.
   c. They can share with their friends.
   d. They can share with the general public.

   ____

   ____

3. **a.** Someone placed the patient's name on a waiting list.
   b. The waiting list was for a transplant.
   c. Details appeared on the screen.
   d. The details were about a matching donor.
   e. It was just a few minutes later.

   ____

   ____

ACTIVITY 9 Steps to Composing

Read the paragraph. Then follow the directions in the 10 steps to edit the information and composition of the paragraph. Write your revised paragraph on a separate sheet of paper. Be careful with capitalization and punctuation. Check your answers with the class.

SUMMARY PARAGRAPH

Media Habits of Students

[1] We conducted a survey of 100 students at Downtown University. [2] We asked students about their media habits, specifically about print versus online sources of news. [3] You can see these results in table 1.1. [4] We found that nearly all students have access to the Internet at home (95 percent). [5] Most students also have Internet access at college (86 percent), on their cell phones (75 percent), or in public places with Wi-Fi like coffee shops (60 percent). [6] Most students (63 percent) are online for more than three hours a day. [7] Eighty-six percent of students say they get news from Web sites. [8] That is not surprising. [9] In fact, 81 percent of the respondents say they use newspaper Web sites for news. [10] Seventy-five percent of the students read the newspaper at least occasionally. [11] No one reads it every day.

1. Change sentence 1 to passive voice to avoid using *we*. Writers sometimes use *we* in describing research, but it is less common.
2. Change sentence 2 to passive voice.
3. Combine sentences 1 and 2. Start with *In a recent survey of.*
4. In sentence 3, avoid addressing the reader as *you*, by changing to passive voice.
5. In sentence 4, avoid using *we*. Make the sentence passive by beginning *It was found that.*
6. Sentence 5 would sound better with a transition word. Use *moreover.*
7. Combine sentences 7 and 8. Begin with *It is not surprising that.*
8. There is a causal relationship between sentences 5 and 6, and sentences 7 and 8. Use a cause and effect transition to introduce your new sentence beginning *It is not surprising that* (e.g., *Therefore, As a result, So*).
9. Combine sentences 10 and 11 with a subordinator that shows contrast.
10. To increase variety, rewrite *Seventy-five percent* as a fraction.

ACTIVITY 10 Original Writing

On a separate sheet of paper, write a paragraph (at least seven sentences) to summarize the results of a study or survey. You can write a summary of the survey results in figure 1, conduct your own survey, or find a study online about a topic that interests you. Use at least one example of the passive voice and underline it; try to use two if possible.

Here are some examples of how to begin.

- *In a survey conducted at* ________________, *students were asked about* ________________.
- *In a study published in* ________________, *researchers found that* ________________.
- *The research, published in* ________________, *suggests that* ________________.

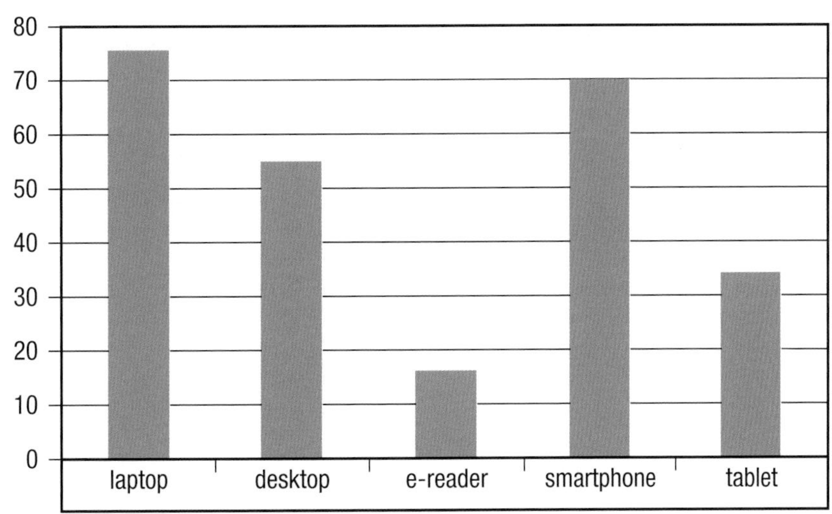

Figure 1: A survey on technology use: Percentage of students who use each device
Respondents: 1,000 adult ESL students
Researchers: Baker County Community College

This photo from the 1940s shows what the American Dream was at the time: a family, a house, and a car.

9 Writing with Participial Adjectives

WHAT DO YOU KNOW?

DISCUSS Look at the photo and read the caption. Discuss the questions.

1. How would you describe the American Dream of today?
2. How do you think a college-age person imagines the American Dream? Would it differ from that of a middle-aged person?

FIND THE ERRORS This paragraph contains two errors with participial adjectives. Find the errors and correct them. Explain your corrections to a partner.

OPINION PARAGRAPH

The American Dream

[1] The American Dream is a traditional American value. [2] It holds that all persons, regardless of their origins, have the chance to move up in society by working hard and taking risks. [3] A 2015 poll sponsored by the *Atlantic* magazine and the Aspen Institute surveyed Americans in four age groups about the American Dream. [4] The survey provided some interested information about the millennial generation, that is, people born between 1980 and 2000. [5] For example, only 22 percent of millennials said that helping other people was their most important goal, the lowest percentage in any age group. [6] In contrast, 46 percent said that they would not be fulfilled unless they had a job that paid a lot of money. [7] Thirty-two percent said that having luxury items was an essential part of the American Dream for them. [8] Millennials are more optimistic about attaining the American Dream than other age groups. [9] These findings appear to support the stereotype of millennials as self-absorbing and very focused on making money.

Grammar Forms

9.1 Present Participial Adjectives

The present participle is the *-ing* form of a verb. Present participles are sometimes used as adjectives.

Form	Example
verb + *-ing*	an **amusing** story a **growing** number of voters

9.2 Past Participial Adjectives

The past participle of a regular verb is the *-ed* form. Past participles are sometimes used as adjectives.

Form	Example
regular verb + *-ed*	a group of **concerned** citizens a **bored** audience
irregular verb form	a **written** agreement The work is **done**.

Notes

1. See Appendix 4, Irregular Verbs, page 230 for a list of past participles.
2. Participial adjectives most commonly come before a noun.
   Though the crime was seen by many people, there were no **known** suspects.
   It was an **interesting** problem, with no clear solution.
3. Participial adjectives can also occur as a complement of *be* or another linking verb, such as *feel, seem, look,* or *taste.*
   Astronaut Chris Hadfield's photos of Earth **are astonishing** in their color and detail.
   At the end of the course, 90 percent of the students said they **felt satisfied**.

ACTIVITY 1

Underline the present or past participial adjectives in each sentence. Do not underline participles that are not adjectives. There may be more than one in a sentence.

1. Heart disease is the leading cause of death in most countries worldwide.
2. Written language was first invented in Mesopotamia around 5000 years ago.
3. Broken bones, or fractures, are common in childhood and often occur when children are playing or participating in sports.
4. The audience loved the performance, which included an amazing group of young acrobats.
5. According to popular folklore, if you make a wish when you see a shooting star, your wish will come true.
6. In 2016, scientists at Wake Forest Medical Center used a 3-D printer to create living tissue to replace damaged or injured body parts.
7. The survey showed that a decreasing number of college students are majoring in languages and literature.
8. Sloths are extremely slow-moving mammals that live in the jungles of Central and South America and mainly eat leaves.

A young three-toed sloth hangs from a branch in a jungle in Costa Rica.

Common Uses

9.3 Using Participial Adjectives

Use	Example
1. Present participial adjectives are usually used when there is an active or continuous meaning.	**running** water (water that is running) **aching** back (a back that is aches)
2. Past participial adjectives are usually used when there is a passive meaning.	**forgotten** memories (forgotten by people) **burned** building (burned by something or someone)
3. When the participial adjective is referring to emotions or feelings:	
a. use the present participle to describe the emotional characteristic of something (or someone, but often a thing or idea)	Shakespeare wrote **entertaining** plays. The news was **distressing**.
b. use the past participle to describe people (or animals; often living) and how they felt	The audience was **entertained**. **Distressed** tigers in zoos may exhibit repetitive behaviors.

ACTIVITY 2

Underline the correct participial adjective in parentheses in each sentence.

1. Since the 2008 recession, more Americans are buying (*using / used*) cars.
2. This research paper reports on statistical methods for dealing with (*missing / missed*) data in a research project.
3. Several devices exist that can help car owners and police track and recover (*stealing / stolen*) vehicles.
4. So far, about 1.2 million species of plants and animals are (*knowing / known*) to science, according to *National Geographic* magazine.
5. Nowadays, many (*publishing / published*) books are available in both print and electronic versions.
6. A (*growing / grown*) number of complications has been discovered in babies born to mothers who contracted the virus.
7. An (*interesting / interested*) new study on diet and nutrition reveals that eating low-fat foods may not be as healthy as previously thought.
8. The newly (*discovering / discovered*) species is a type of dragonfly. An article about this (*fascinating / fascinated*) discovery can be found on the museum's website.

Common Errors

Common Error 9.1 Do you need a present or past participle?

Pascal Cotte, a French scientist who used reflective light technology to study the *Mona Lisa*, was ~~surprising~~ surprised to discover another portrait underneath the Da Vinci masterpiece.

REMEMBER: When the participial adjective involves feeling or emotion, use the past participle to describe how someone feels or felt. Use the present participle to describe the emotional characteristic of something or someone.

ACTIVITY 3 Common Error 9.1

For each sentence, fill in the blank with the correct present or past participial adjective of the verb in parentheses.

1. When people are ____________________ (*depress*), some experience a loss of appetite, while others report that they cannot stop eating.
2. Though the idea was ____________________ (*interest*) to many, it was not enough to sustain a two and a half hour movie. In online reviews, many moviegoers said that they were ____________________ (*bore*) after one hour.
3. The ____________________ (*devastate*) situation in the war-torn country has left many families broken. Volunteer psychologists have come to the camp to work with ____________________ (*trouble*) children.
4. The *Hollywood Reporter* described the 2015 movie *American Ultra*, starring Kristen Stewart and Jesse Eisenberg, as "mildly ____________________ (*amuse*)."
5. Therapy and treatment were recommended for the ____________________ (*traumatize*) victims of the earthquake.
6. The patient was ____________________ (*concern*) about the results and decided to seek a second opinion.
7. A ____________________ (*grow*) number of apps enable people in cities to save money by finding travelers who will share a cab with them.
8. New York's High Line park was built on an ____________________ (*elevate*) section of an ____________________ (*abandon*) railroad line.

Common Error 9.2 Do you have the correct participial form?

The FDA recommends that people do not leave ~~cook~~ *cooked* eggs out of the refrigerator for more than two hours.

REMEMBER: Use the correct form of a present or past participle.

ACTIVITY 4 Common Error 9.2

For each sentence, find the incorrect form for a participle. Write the correct participle above the word.

1. Distract driving is any activity that can take a driver's attention away from the task of driving. Texting is the most alarm distraction because it involves not only the driver's eyes but also the hands and the brain.
2. In the 2012 Olympic swimming competition, Daniel Gyurta of Hungary won the 200-meter men's breaststroke race with an astonish time of 2 minutes, 7.28 seconds.
3. Recently there have been grow demands for the senator to resign.
4. Last winter's freeze temperatures and record snowfall have had a negative effect on this summer's apple harvest.
5. Managers in large companies need to have a strategic approach to managing stress employees.
6. An increase number of people are buying fresh produce at a local farmers' market.
7. The complete bridge will connect the village to larger commercial areas.
8. It was a very complicating experiment and required a very detailed analysis of the data.
9. A customer who is satisfy is very likely to buy from that business again.
10. For a very limit time, travelers can purchase reduced air fares for many destinations.

Academic Vocabulary

Participial Adjectives Frequently Used in Academic Writing

Present		Past	
developing	growing	concerned	involved
existing	interesting	gifted	limited
following		increased	

Source: *A comparative analysis of present and past participial adjectives and their collocations in the Corpus of Contemporary American English (COCA)* (Reilly 2013)

ACTIVITY 5 Vocabulary in Academic Writing

Use the academic vocabulary words to complete the sentences.

Subject Area	Example from Academic Writing
Medicine	**1.** In patients aged 70 and older, high monthly doses of vitamin D were associated with a(n) ________________ risk of falling.
Nutrition	**2.** Eating meat is becoming more popular in China. At the same time, a ________________ number of young people, mainly in large cities, have started following a vegan diet.
Marketing	**3.** The goal of the present study is to add to the small amount of ________________ knowledge concerning the daily use of mineral water by ordinary consumers.
Music	**4.** Joshua Bell, recognized as one of the most ________________ violin players in the world, began taking violin lessons at the age of four.
Public Health	**5.** Many people in ________________ nations such as Thailand often cannot afford dental care. Many reach adulthood without ever seeing a dentist or dental hygienist.
Education	**6.** Students who are ________________ in community service activities such as volunteering tend to do better in school, perhaps because volunteering gives them the chance to apply the skills they learn in the classroom.
Sociology	**7.** A(n) ________________ finding of the study was that people tend to choose marriage partners with DNA that is similar to theirs.
Urban Planning	**8.** Throughout Los Angeles, ________________ homeowners are attending meetings to discuss ways to control the building of oversized homes known as McMansions.
Geography	**9.** The Arabian Peninsula includes the ________________ countries: Saudi Arabia, Yemen, Oman, Bahrain, Kuwait, Qatar, and the United Arab Emirates.
Economics	**10.** Competition generally increases as a result of ________________ resources.

Put It Together

ACTIVITY 6 Review Quiz

Multiple Choice Choose the letter of the correct answer.

1. There are more than 7,000 ______ languages in existence today.

   a. living **b.** lived

2. After meditating, the anxious children became more ______ and were better able to focus in class.

   a. relaxing **b.** relaxed

3. The musical's engagement at a Broadway theater in New York City was canceled after ______ ticket sales and negative reviews.

   a. disappointing **b.** disappointed

4. In an ______ article in the journal *Nature*, scientists at the University of California, Irvine, described a wearable plastic patch that can measure levels of glucose, salt, and other minerals in a person's sweat.

   a. interesting **b.** interested

5. When Igor Stravinsky's ballet *The Rite of Spring* debuted in Paris on May 29, 1913, ______ audience members shouted and threw things at the dancers.

   a. shocking **b.** shocked

Error Correction One of the five underlined words or phrases is not correct. Find the error and correct it. Be prepared to explain your answer.

6. The impulse to run or drive away from a flood is understandable but unwise because as little as six inches (15 centimeters) of risen water can knock a person over, while just 18 inches (46 centimeters) of moving water can carry away a car.

7. Please note that while the campus police make every effort to identify and contact the owners of found property that has been turned in, we cannot be responsible for lost or damaging items in our possession.

8. Children learn spoken language by exposure, without specific instruction; but writing language is an invented representation of the spoken word that must be taught.

Technicians at the NASA Kennedy Space Center in Florida test a Mars Exploration rover.

ACTIVITY 7 **Building Greater Sentences**

Combine these short sentences into one sentence. You can add new words and move words around, but you should not add or omit any ideas. More than one answer is possible, but the sentences require participial adjectives.

1. **a.** The Mars Exploration Rover mission (MER) is a space mission.
b. It is ongoing.
c. It involves two vehicles.
d. They are robotic.
e. Their purpose is to explore the surface of the planet Mars.

2. **a.** The United Kingdom of Great Britain and Northern Ireland is in Europe.
b. It is commonly called the U.K. or Britain for short.
c. It consists of four countries.
d. The countries are England, Scotland, Wales, and Northern Ireland.

3. **a.** In 2006, archaeologists were excavating a 4,000-year-old settlement in the Qinghai Province.
b. The province is near the Tibetan border.
c. They uncovered an ancient bowl of noodles.
d. The bowl was buried under 10 feet (3 meters) of earth.

ACTIVITY 8 Steps to Composing

Read the essay. Then follow the directions in the 10 steps below to edit the information and composition of the essay. Write your revised essay on a separate sheet of paper. Be careful with capitalization and punctuation. Check your answers with the class.

SUMMARY ESSAY

Millennials and Marriage

[1] Fewer and fewer young Americans are getting married. [2] This is according to a 2014 report by the Pew Research Center. [3] Fewer young people are getting married. [4] Many are also getting married later. [5] Twenty-five percent of millennials—those who were born between 1980 and 2000—will never marry, according to the report.

[6] Three main reasons explain why the number of married people is falling. [7] Thirty percent of those who participated in the survey said that they had not found the right person. [8] Twenty-seven percent said that they were not financially prepared to get married. [9] And 22 percent said that they simply did not feel ready to get married.

[10] Another reason for the marriage rate is related to the employment status of today's young men and women. [11] Most women want to marry a man with a secure job. [12] However, according to the Pew report, millennial men are less likely to be employed than they were in past decades. [13] At the same time, more and more women are entering the labor force, with the result that there are more single, employed young women than single, employed young men. [14] In the future, women who are having trouble finding a suitable marriage partner may elect to marry men who are divorced, widowed, or older.

1. In sentence 1, change *fewer and fewer* to *a decreasing number of* for a more academic tone.
2. Combine sentences 1 and 2. Begin with the information in 2 to make the research more prominent.
3. Combine sentences 3 and 4 with *not only . . . but also*. Make necessary changes to punctuation and word order.
4. Insert *In fact* at the beginning of sentence 5.
5. In sentence 6, change *why the number of married people is falling* to *the falling number of married people*.

6. In sentence 7, change the phrase *those who participated* to *the participants.*

7. In sentences 8 and 9, replace *said* with synonyms. Use a different synonym in each sentence to avoid repetition.

8. Sentence 9 begins with *and*, which is acceptable in spoken English but not in written English. Combine sentences 8 and 9.

9. In sentence 10, insert *falling* in front of the word *marriage.*

10. In sentence 13, replace *more and more* with *a growing number of* for a more academic tone.

ACTIVITY 9 Original Writing

On a separate sheet of paper, write a short summary (at least seven sentences) of a meeting, survey, study, or research report in the academic field of your choice. Use at least one present or past participial adjective; underline it. Try to use two if possible.

Here are some examples of how to begin.

- *On May 10, the Department of Political Science and International Relations sponsored a panel discussion on ways to bridge the digital divide between developed and developing countries.*
- *A study published by the University of London reports that dogs are able to recognize human emotions by combining information from different senses. Until now, only humans were known to have this ability.*
- *An increasing number of female physicians are becoming anesthesiologists, but they earn significantly less than their male colleagues, according to a RAND Corporation study.*

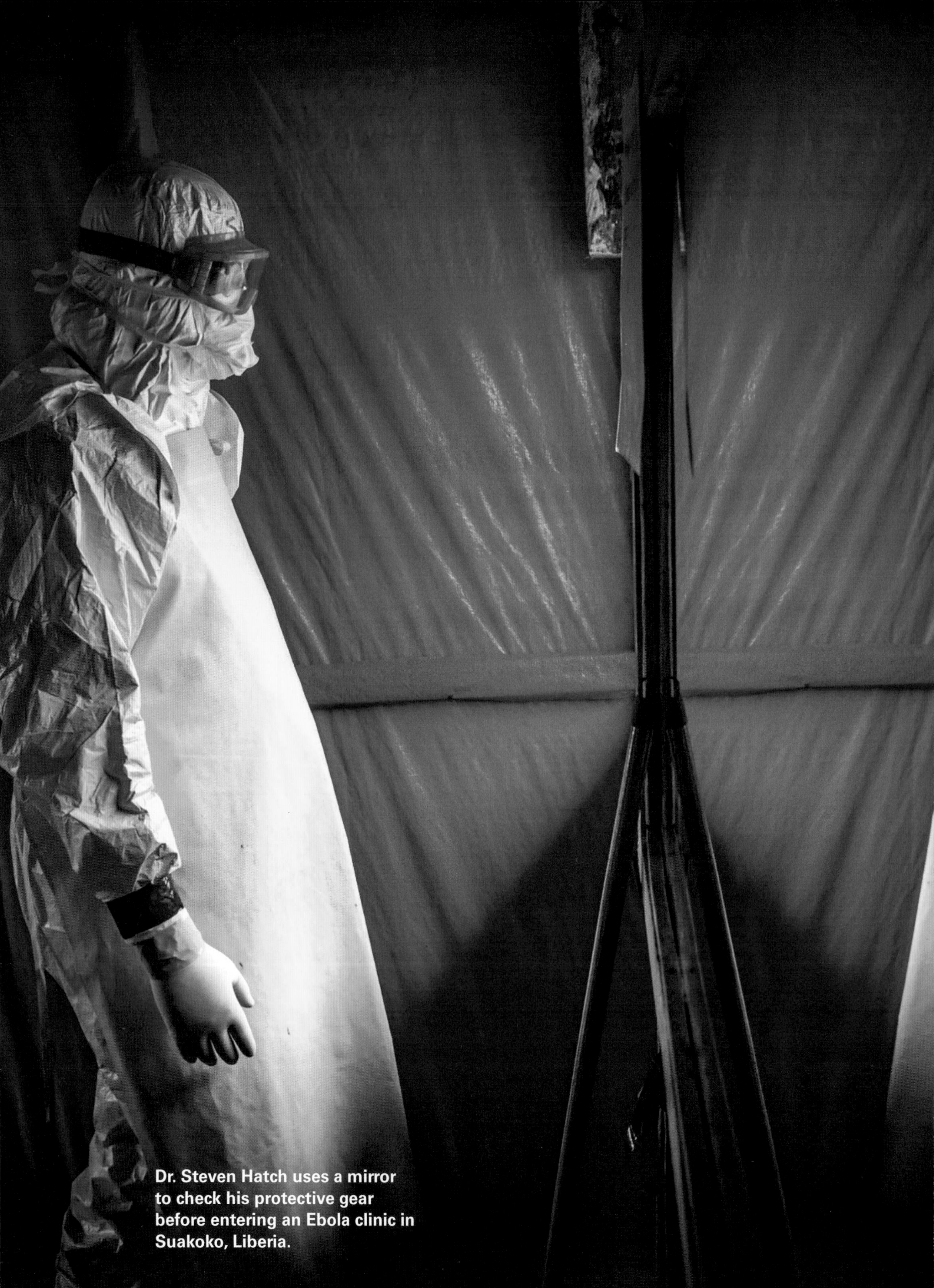

Dr. Steven Hatch uses a mirror to check his protective gear before entering an Ebola clinic in Suakoko, Liberia.

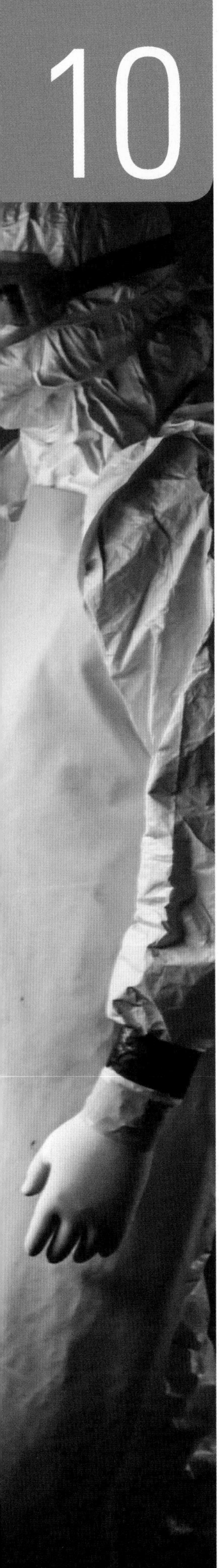

10 Adjective Clauses and Reduced Adjective Clauses

WHAT DO YOU KNOW?

DISCUSS Look at the photo and read the caption. Discuss the questions.

1. Why is this doctor dressed like this?
2. What are some diseases that are highly contagious?

FIND THE ERRORS This paragraph contains two errors with adjective clauses. Find the errors and correct them. Explain your corrections to a partner.

CAUSE–EFFECT PARAGRAPH

Ebola

[1] Ebola, which is also known as Ebola hemorrhagic fever or Ebola virus disease, is a disease spreads when a person comes into contact with body fluids of an infected person or animal. [2] Symptoms include a fever, a sore throat, and headaches, and usually start between 2 and 21 days after exposure. [3] To control the spread of this deadly disease, people who they are exposed are kept in quarantine for three weeks. [4] If they show no symptoms during that time, they are not likely to contract the disease. [5] Although often fatal, recovery is in fact possible if the infected person receives proper medical treatment quickly enough. [6] Between 2013 and 2016, Ebola spread throughout West Africa. [7] This outbreak was traced back to a one-year-old child who lived in Guinea. [8] Within a relatively short time, the disease spread to Liberia and Sierra Leone. [9] This Ebola outbreak became the largest ever recorded.

Grammar Forms

10.1 Adjective Clauses

Like other clauses, an adjective clause (also called a relative clause) has a subject and a verb. Like adjectives, adjective clauses modify a noun or noun phrase. An adjective clause usually comes after the noun it modifies and begins with a relative pronoun (*that, who, whom,* or *which*). Adjective clauses are dependent clauses. There are two main patterns of adjective clauses.

Pattern	Example
1. Subject adjective clause relative pronoun + verb The relative pronoun is the subject of the clause.	S V Transpiration is a process **that involves** plants. | independent clause | | adjective clause |
2. Object adjective clause relative pronoun + subject + verb The relative pronoun is the object of the clause. Object relative pronouns may be omitted.	O S V Transpiration is a process **(that) plants use** for | independent clause | | adjective clause | cooling.

Notes

1. The verb in a subject adjective clause agrees with the noun being modified.
   Transpiration is a process **that involves plants**.
   The plants **that grow in the desert** have to be drought tolerant.
2. Adjective clauses are dependent clauses. They can come after any noun in a sentence.
   The police are investigating the fire **that damaged several buildings last week.**
3. The adjective clause can also come between the subject and the verb of the independent clause. In this case, make sure the subject and verb of the independent clause agree.
   The fire **that damaged several buildings last week** was the result of arson.
4. The relative pronoun takes the place of a subject or object in the clause. Therefore, do *not* add a subject or object pronoun to the clause.
   Transpiration is a process **that ~~it~~ involves plants**.
   Transpiration is a process **that plants use ~~it~~ for cooling**.

10.2 Reduced Subject Adjective Clauses

Many subject adjective clauses can be reduced or shortened. There are two patterns:

Pattern	Example
1. In clauses with the verb *be*, omit the relative pronoun and the verb *be*.	The fish ~~that is~~ upsetting the local ecosystem is known as the snakehead fish. The fish **upsetting the local ecosystem** is known as the snakehead fish.

10.2 Reduced Subject Adjective Clauses (Continued)

2. With some verbs other than *be*, omit the relative pronoun and add *-ing* to the base form of the verb. • In the negative form, *not* comes before the verb.	Anyone ~~who wants~~ to be a commercial pilot must have at least 250 hours of flight time. Anyone **wanting to be a commercial pilot** must have at least 250 hours of flight time. Anyone **not wanting to be disappointed** should register for the event soon.

ACTIVITY 1

Underline the correct verb forms to complete the sentences. Then rewrite each sentence so the subject adjective clause is reduced. The first one is done for you.

1. Countries that (*borders* / *border*) the equator (*has* / *have*) extremely high temperatures.

   Countries bordering the equator have extremely high temperatures.

2. The person who (*was* / *were*) honored at the ceremony started one of the biggest companies in Silicon Valley.

   ____

   ____

3. Cars that (*runs* / *run*) on electricity (*saves* / *save*) gas and are highly praised by environmentalists.

   ____

   ____

4. Researchers who (*is* / *are*) trying to find a cure for cancer sometimes (*works* / *work*) at large research universities such as Stanford, Yale, or Johns Hopkins.

   ____

   ____

5. The Nobel Prizes that (*is* / *are*) awarded each year (*is* / *are*) for physics, chemistry, medicine, and literature.

   ____

   ____

6. The number of women who (*goes* / *go*) to school in Afghanistan (*has* / *have*) increased by

over 30 percent since 2002.

7. A panda that (*lives / live*) in a zoo (*has / have*) a longer life span than one in the wild.

8. Tourists who (*visits / visit*) Beijing's Forbidden City can see the inside of the imperial palace.

9. Birds that do not (*migrate / migrates*) south (*is / are*) able to find enough food throughout the year.

10. Teachers who (*flip / flips*) their classrooms (*has / have*) moved traditional lectures out of the classroom.

ACTIVITY 2

Underline the three subject adjective clauses and reduce them. Underline the three object adjective clauses and reduce them by deleting the relative pronoun.

Stop the Speeding

According to the Department of Transportation, speeding is a deadly habit that accounts for about a third of all automobile accidents in the United States. What do most of the drivers who are caught driving so fast give as their excuse? The number one excuse that these drivers give is that they are late for some extremely important event. Most police officers are used to hearing this unoriginal excuse, so they do not accept it as a valid reason. Drivers who do not pay attention to the speed limit should have to pay a high fine for the potentially dangerous situation that they have created. Putting innocent people at risk because of an inability to manage time is unacceptable, and it is certainly something that the police and transportation laws must be able to discourage.

Common Uses

10.3 Using Adjective Clauses

Adjective clauses are commonly used in writing. They are used:

1. to connect ideas or to avoid short sentences	Helen Keller was a young woman. She faced many challenges. Helen Keller was a young woman **who faced many challenges**. Visuals can enhance a presentation. They should relate to the information in the text. Visuals **that relate to the information in the text** can enhance a presentation.
2. to describe a person **a.** use **who** or **that** for a subject	Jane Austen is the famous 18th century British author **who / that** wrote *Emma*.
b. use **whom** or **that** for an object; note that *who* is often used in less formal writing, but *whom* is preferred in academic writing. • When the relative pronoun is an object, it may be omitted.	Rosa Parks is the civil rights activist **whom / that** the police arrested for refusing to give up her bus seat. Rosa Parks is the activist the police arrested for refusing to give up her bus seat. (Relative pronoun *whom / that* is omitted.)
3. to describe a thing or animal **a.** use **that** or **which** for a subject	Peru is a country **that / which** is located in South America between Chile and Ecuador.
b. use **that** or **which** for an object • When the relative pronoun is an object, it may be omitted.	Peru is a South American country **that / which** millions visit each year. Peru is a South American country millions visit each year. (Relative pronoun *that / which* is omitted.)
4. to add extra information about a noun **a.** Restrictive: the information in the adjective clause is essential to the meaning and is not set off with a comma or commas.	According to a survey by a national association, the ice cream flavor **that is ordered most often** is vanilla.
b. Nonrestrictive: the information in the adjective clause is not essential to the meaning and is set off with a comma or commas. Never use *that* after a comma in a nonrestrictive clause.	Vanilla is more popular than chocolate, **which is people's number two choice according to the survey**.
5. to make writing more concise and sound more academic	Mint marks are small initials **stamped on** coins to indicate where a coin was produced. (Reduced from *that are stamped on*.)

ACTIVITY 3

Use the information in the second sentence to write a new sentence with a subject or object adjective clause. Use the relative pronoun provided in parentheses.

1. Zebras live only in zoos.

These zebras live outside of Africa.

(*that*) ______________________________

____

2. Those bright pink birds are called Roseate spoonbills.

Many people have spotted the bright pink birds near the lake.

(*which*) ______________________________

____

3. Some people recycle more than others.

These people are concerned about the environment.

(*who*) ______________________________

____

4. The survey result indicated that college students now prefer to communicate via social media.

This survey result interested us the most.

(*that*) ______________________________

____

5. Snowstorms have the potential to cause many deaths.

These snowstorms produce avalanches.

(*that*) ______________________________

____

6. Exotic pets can harm an ecosystem by eating native animals' food.

People illegally release their exotic pets.

(*that*) ______________________________

____

ACTIVITY 4

Combine the two sentences to write a sentence with a nonrestrictive adjective clause. Use a correct relative pronoun and correct punctuation.

1. Alaska is home to surprisingly few people. Alaska is the largest U.S. state in terms of size.

2. The liberal Supreme Court Justice Ruth Bader Ginsburg considered Antonin Scalia a great friend. Justice Antonin Scalia was very conservative.

3. Galileo Galilei has been called the father of science. Galileo Galilei discovered four of Jupiter's moons.

4. Toyota was the first company to release a hybrid car. Toyota was founded in 1937.

5. The city plans to update Beach Park. Many people love Beach Park for its trails.

6. Benazir Bhutto was the prime minister of Pakistan between 1988 and 1990 and between 1993 and 1996. Bhutto was born in Karachi.

Common Errors

Common Error 10.1 Do you need a subject relative pronoun?

that
A university major ^ deals with any aspect of business is likely to result in much higher lifetime earnings.

REMEMBER: Do not forget to use a relative pronoun in the subject position.

ACTIVITY 5 Common Error 10.1

Read the following sentences. If an adjective clause is missing a relative pronoun, write *X* on the line. Then write a pronoun above the sentence. More than one pronoun may be correct. If the pronoun is not missing, write *C* on the line.

_______ **1.** The millions of tourists visited Florida last year contributed more than 20 percent of the state's annual sales tax revenue.

_______ **2.** Although not many people know it, coins bear the letter D were produced in the city of Denver.

_______ **3.** The chakana is a symbol that orginated in South America.

_______ **4.** Terns are a type of seabird can be found on beaches worldwide.

_______ **5.** Alternative medicine is a practice that makes use of nontraditional types of medicine.

_______ **6.** Physics is a field of natural science studies the way matter moves through space and time.

_______ **7.** A production process that could produce aluminum inexpensively was not invented until the 1880s.

_______ **8.** *War and Peace* is a novel names approximately 160 real people within its pages.

Common Error 10.2 Do you have the correct relative pronoun?

which
The state of California, ~~that~~ was the most populous state in the country in 2014, is located on the west coast of the United States.

REMEMBER: Use *who, that,* or *whom* for people and *that* or *which* for things. Do not use *that* in nonrestrictive clauses. Do not use *whom* in a subject adjective clause.

ACTIVITY 6 Common Error 10.2

Read each sentence. Fill in the blank with the correct relative pronoun: *who*, *whom*, *that*, or *which*. More than one answer may be possible.

1. Paris is a popular tourist destination ____________________ around 27 million people visit each year.
2. The Golden Gate Bridge, ____________________ is located in San Francisco, is one of the most photographed bridges in the world.
3. Ansel Adams, ____________________ photographed the American West, focused a great deal of his work on Yosemite National Park.
4. In 2011, Bollywood sold over 3.5 billion tickets, ____________________ was 900,000 more than Hollywood.
5. A welder is a person ____________________ specializes in fusing pieces of metal or plastic together.
6. The hospital dismissed the doctor ____________________ the court found guilty of fraud.
7. Maria Montessori, ____________________ was born in Italy, opened a childcare center in Rome where she could practice her educational theories.
8. Incandescent light bulbs have a wire filament ____________________ is heated by an electric current until the light is visible to the naked eye.

Common Error 10.3 Do you repeat the subject or object pronoun?

University students that ~~they~~ attend graduate school might be asked to write a paper with both primary and secondary sources.

Books and interviews are examples of sources that writers should include ~~them~~.

REMEMBER: In an adjective clause, do not include a pronoun that refers to the modified noun. The subject relative pronoun (*that*, *who*, or *which*) or the object relative pronoun (*that*, *whom*, or *which*) is all that is needed.

ACTIVITY 7 Common Error 10.3

Read each sentence. Cross out the unnecessary pronoun in each.

1. For a wide variety of reasons, George Washington is the U.S. president that historians praise him most for his contributions to the young nation.
2. Although Benjamin Franklin is of course known for his work in international politics, an area of science that he investigated it a great deal was electricity.
3. The issues that they resonate most with voters this year are trustworthiness and the economy.
4. Venus, which it is the closest planet to Earth, is named after the Roman goddess of love and beauty.
5. The land that the Spaniard Juan Diaz de Solis explored it in 1516 is in present day Uruguay.
6. Smartphones are one of the gadgets that they made the list of devices people say they cannot live without.

Common Error 10.4 Is the subject adjective clause reduced correctly?

The end of the U.S. Civil War, ~~which~~ fought between the North and the South, resulted in freedom for the slaves.

REMEMBER: Both the relative pronoun and the *be* verb need to be deleted.

ACTIVITY 8 Common Error 10.4

Each sentence has an error. Cross out the subject relative pronouns or *be* verbs that need to be deleted to make a correct reduced clause.

1. French impressionism, which founded by artists in the 19th century, faced criticism from the traditional artists in France.
2. Reindeer, which first noted by Aristotle in writings from 350 BCE, probably referred to a deer species named *tarandos*.
3. Technology changes quickly, and cell phones were developed last year are already considered outdated.
4. Tagalog, is spoken in the Philippines, is also used by inhabitants on the islands of Lubang, Marinduque, and Mindoro.
5. *Death of a Salesman,* which written in 1949 by Arthur Miller, is still representative of the modern-day pursuit of the American Dream.
6. Rapid transit systems, which also known as metros or subways, include the world's largest network, the Greater Tokyo rail system.

Academic Vocabulary

Nouns That Frequently Precede Adjective Clauses with *That* in Academic Writing

activity	area	idea	issue	organization
approach	element	indication	option	result

Source: Corpus of Contemporary American English (Davies 2008)

ACTIVITY 9 Vocabulary in Academic Writing

Use the academic vocabulary words to complete the sentences. More than one answer may be possible.

Subject Area	Example from Academic Writing
Political Science	**1.** According to the nation's president, improving the jobless rate is a(n) ________________ that his administration will focus on if he is re-elected for a second term.
Business Management	**2.** Teamwork is one ________________ that companies try in order to help people feel they are part of a group and to lead to better work overall; therefore, it is a much better way than having people work individually.
English Composition	**3.** The Salvation Army is a large ________________ that aims to advance education and relieve poverty as part of its mission.
Geology	**4.** The coastal region of California is the ________________ that geologists need to study more thoroughly to determine the effects of global warming on rising sea levels.
Chemistry	**5.** Potassium is the ________________ that Sir Humphry Davy first isolated at the Royal Institution in London.
Social Studies	**6.** The number of violent crimes committed by teens who play video games is a(n) ________________ that parents should be aware of.
Law	**7.** The guilty verdict was the ________________ that the legal team hoped for at the end of the six-month-long trial.
Education	**8.** Using authentic materials in the classroom is a(n) ________________ that more and more teachers support.
Computer Science	**9.** Debugging the software program is the ________________ that takes longer but is less expensive than coding an entirely new program.
Health	**10.** Walking is a very important ________________ that many physical therapy programs incorporate to help patients recuperating from knee surgery.

Put It Together

ACTIVITY 10 Review Quiz

Multiple Choice Choose the letter of the correct answer.

1. Beethoven's Symphony Number 5, ______ was written in the early 1800s, is still one of the most frequently played pieces of classical music.

   a. which **b.** that **c.** who **d.** whom

2. Adam Smith, ______ is considered a leader in the field of economics, wrote *The Wealth of Nations*.

   a. which **b.** that **c.** who **d.** whom

3. The Battle of Verdun, ______ one of the largest battles of World War I, led to more than 714,000 casualties in 1916.

   a. that was **b.** was **c.** which was **d.** been

4. Reproductions of Monet's works, ______ *Water Lilies*, can be found in stores around the world.

   a. that they include **b.** including **c.** they include **d.** include

5. Saudi Arabia is a country ______ seven other countries: Iraq, Jordan, Kuwait, Yemen, Oman, Qatar, and the United Arab Emirates.

   a. borders **b.** that borders **c.** bordered **d.** what borders

Error Correction One of the five underlined words or phrases is not correct. Find the error and correct it. Be prepared to explain your answer.

6. The respiratory system, which is responsible for taking in oxygen and getting rid of carbon dioxide, are subject to several diseases or conditions ranging from pneumonia to asthma.

7. Statistics show that fibromyalgia, that is a disorder affecting the musculoskeletal system, has different effects on women, who are much more likely to have this disease.

8. The office in charge of federal and state elections in California prepares voter information in many languages, which tests all voting equipment, and makes sure that every vote is counted.

The ancient Topkapi Palace in Istanbul, Turkey, was used as a royal residence from 1465 until 1856.

ACTIVITY 11 Building Greater Sentences

Combine these short sentences into one sentence. You can add new words and move words around, but you should not add or omit any ideas. More than one answer is possible, but these sentences require adjective clauses.

1. **a.** Mustafa Kemal Atatürk founded Turkey.
b. Turkey was founded in 1923.
c. Mustafa Kemal Atatürk helped Turkey with political reforms.

2. **a.** Benjamin Franklin helped negotiate the Treaty of Paris in 1783.
b. He was born in Boston in 1706.
c. The treaty led to the end of the Revolutionary War.

3. **a.** The nose is the main opening for the body's respiratory system.
b. The nose is made of cartilage, bone, muscle, and skin.
c. The respiratory system provides oxygen to the body while removing carbon dioxide.

ACTIVITY 12 Steps to Composing

Read the paragraph. Then follow the directions in the 10 steps to edit the information and composition of the paragraph. Write your revised paragraph on a separate sheet of paper. Be careful with capitalization and punctuation. Check your answers with the class.

NARRATIVE PARAGRAPH

Helen Keller

[1] Helen Keller was a young woman. [2] She faced many challenges. [3] She was deaf, mute, and blind. [4] Despite her challenges, she learned how to communicate thanks to a good teacher. [5] Anne Sullivan was her teacher. [6] Anne came to the United States from Ireland in the 1840s. [7] She grew up very poor and actually had her own vision problems. [8] She suffered from an eye disease called trachoma. [9] Trachoma is an eye infection that can lead to blindness. [10] It usually occurs when people live in impoverished conditions and have limited water and health care. [11] Sullivan went to a school for the blind and had surgery to correct her limited vision. [12] While at the school, the director helped her find a job. [13] He was named Michael Anagnos. [14] Michael put her in contact with the Keller family. [15] Then Sullivan moved to Alabama to work with Helen Keller. [16] It was Helen Keller who made Sullivan famous. [17] That was the beginning of a famous student-teacher relationship in history.

1. The first two sentences are short and sound very abrupt. Combine these into one longer sentence using an adjective clause.
2. Sentences 5 and 6 both talk about the teacher. Use an adjective clause to combine them.
3. In sentence 6, change the verb *came* to a verb with a more specific meaning.
4. Both sentences 8 and 9 talk about trachoma, which was her medical condition. Use an adjective clause to combine them.
5. In sentence 10, does the word *it* refer to blindness or trachoma? Because the reference for the pronoun *it* is not clear, change *it* to a noun.
6. In sentence 11, the verb *went* is a weak verb. Change *went* to another verb with a more concrete meaning.
7. Both sentences 12 and 13 talk about the director. Use an adjective clause to combine them.

8. The word *then* in sentence 15 is vague. Change it to the year 1887 and make any other necessary changes.

9. Both sentences 15 and 16 refer to Helen Keller. Combine them using an adjective clause.

10. To have a more impressive concluding sentence, change the word *a* to the phrase *one of the most.*

ACTIVITY 13 Original Writing

On a separate sheet of paper, write a narrative paragraph (at least seven sentences) in which you talk about someone famous or someone you know well. Use at least one example of an adjective clause and one reduced adjective clause; try to use two if possible. Underline your examples.

Here are some examples of how to begin.

- *Jeremy Lin, who plays professional basketball, was born in Palo Alto, California.*
- *Former U.S. Secretary of State Madeleine Albright has an immigration story that is very interesting.*
- *The person who most influenced my decision to become an economics major was Adam Smith.*

Dinesh Patel (left) of the Pittsburgh Pirates shares a laugh with a teammate during spring training in 2009 in Florida.

Adverb Clauses and Reduced Adverb Clauses

WHAT DO YOU KNOW?

DISCUSS Look at the photo and read the caption. Discuss the questions.

1. What do you know about American baseball? How is the game played?
2. What is your favorite sport to play or to watch? Why?

FIND THE ERRORS This paragraph contains two errors with adverb clauses. Find the errors and correct them. Explain your corrections to a partner.

DESCRIPTIVE PARAGRAPH

Dinesh Patel

[1] Dinesh Patel is a baseball player who pitched for the Pittsburgh Pirates organization. [2] This does not sound very exciting, he was the first Indian ever to sign a contract with a professional athletic team in the United States. [3] The story of how this happened is unusual. [4] In 2008, Patel and another Indian named Rinku Singh joined an Indian reality television show called *The Million Dollar Arm*, which was created to discover new baseball players. [5] Neither Patel nor Singh had ever played baseball when participated on the show. [6] They beat more than 37,000 competitors to win the chance to try out in front of representatives from professional baseball teams in the United States. [7] They were both signed by the Pittsburg Pirates and played in the minor league. [8] Their success story was the subject of a Walt Disney movie in 2014. [9] Patel and Singh returned to India after playing baseball for one year in America. [10] Even though Patel did not succeed as a major league pitcher in the United States, the experience gave him the skills and income to improve his life and that of his family.

Grammar Forms

11.1 Adverb Clauses

Like other clauses, an adverb clause has a subject and a verb. Adverb clauses are dependent clauses and must be attached to an independent clause.

Pattern	Example		
1. Adverb clauses begin with a subordinating conjunction.	after although as as soon as because before	even though once since so so that though	until when whenever whereas while
2. Sub. Conj. + S + V, Ind. Clause	**Even though** baseball is more widely played in the United States, many say it originated in England. (Sub. Conj. = Even though; S = baseball; V = is)		
3. Ind. Clause + Sub Conj. + S + V	Many say baseball originated in England **even though** it is more widely played in the United States. (Sub. Conj. = even though; S = it; V = is)		

Notes

1. Put a comma after the adverb clause if it begins the sentence.

   So that they will be counted toward the final results, mail-in ballots must be postmarked by a certain date.

   Do not use a comma if the adverb clause comes after the main clause.

   Mail-in ballots must be postmarked by a certain date **so that they will be counted toward the final results**.
2. In academic writing, it is more common to place the adverb clause at the beginning of the sentence.
3. When the conjunction *so* or *so that* introduces an adverb clause of purpose, do not add the comma. In this case, *so that* means the same as *in order that*.

   Mail your ballot early **so that** your vote is counted.

   Mail your ballot early **in order that** your vote is counted.
4. See Appendix 2, Connectors, page 225, for a list of subordinating conjunctions.

11.2 Reduced Adverb Clauses

Many adverb clauses can be reduced or shortened. Reducing is possible when the subject in the adverb clause is the same as the subject in the independent clause, and when one of the following subordinating conjunctions is used: *after, although, before, even if, even though, if, though, unless, until, when, whenever,* and *while.*

1. To reduce an adverb clause with the verb *be,* delete the subject and the form of *be.* You may need to change the subject pronoun in the independent clause to the specific noun.	**When people are stressed,** they exhibit symptoms such as high blood pressure and an accelerated heart rate. **When stressed,** people exhibit symptoms such as high blood pressure and an accelerated heart rate.
2. To reduce an adverb clause of time with a verb other than *be,* omit the subject and change the verb to the *-ing* form. Remember to replace the pronoun with the specific noun, if necessary.	**While people sleep**, they dream four to six times each night. **While sleeping,** people dream four to six times each night.
3. To reduce an adverb clause of reason, omit *since* or *because* and the subject and change the verb to the *-ing* form.	**Because the students had read the lab manual,** they were able to reproduce their professor's results. **Having read the lab manual,** the students were able to reproduce their professor's results.

ACTIVITY 1

Underline the adverb clause in each sentence. Add a comma when necessary.

1. While the National Sleep Foundation recommends adults get 7 to 9 hours of sleep a night it also says 6 or 10 hours may be appropriate.
2. As the presidential campaign continues it is becoming obvious that people are very concerned about environmental issues.
3. The company increased marketing efforts so sales would improve.
4. The treaty took effect because the presidents of the two countries agreed on new import and export taxes.
5. After Arizona joined the United States in 1912 the number of states remained at 48 until 1959.
6. The World Health Organization was called on to investigate so that a similar outbreak might be prevented in the future.
7. Although Levittown is not a municipality it is recognized as Philadelphia's largest suburb.
8. Everyone needs to be aware of building exits even though the need for an evacuation is rare.

ACTIVITY 2

Underline the adverb clause in each sentence. Then write the reduction above it.

1. When people are jetlagged, they may suffer longer depending on how many time zones they have crossed.
2. John McCain became a United States senator after he served in the military.
3. Although a U.S. president is elected in November, he or she does not take office until January.
4. Because they face danger in their own country, people often flee to other countries and become refugees.
5. Dinosaurs lived on the earth for 160 million years before they became extinct.
6. When snakes are molting, they shed their skin, which will be replaced by new skin.
7. Before the polka was introduced in England in the 19th century, it was a popular dance in what was then known as Czechoslovakia.
8. Carrie Underwood became famous after she won the TV contest *American Idol* in 2005.
9. Though Oklahoma was acquired by the United States in 1803, it did not become a state until 1907.
10. Though armadillos are unable to see well, they are good hunters thanks to their fine sense of smell.

Common Uses

11.3 Using Adverb Clauses and Reduced Adverb Clauses

Adverb clauses are commonly used in writing to connect ideas and show logical relationships. In conversation, we tend to use full clauses. In composition, good writers use a variety of sentence structures, including both adverb clauses and reduced adverb clauses. Use subordinating conjunctions to accurately express the relationship between the clauses.

Pattern	Example
1. Reason or cause: Use *because* or *since* before the cause or reason. The effect or result is in the independent clause.	**Because** Charlie Chaplin's father left his family, his mother had to support the family as a singer.
2. Contrast: Use *while, although,* or *whereas* before a statement that contrasts what is in the independent clause.	**While** his mother's career was not prosperous, Chaplin went on to have a longer and more prosperous career.
3. Concession: Use *although, though,* or *even though* before a statement of concession that may be unexpected or surprising.	**Even though** Chaplin was difficult to work with, his films were very successful.
4. Purpose: Use *so that* or *so* to state a purpose, much like *in order to.*	Chaplin visited the United States one last time **so that** he could accept an honorary Academy Award.
5. Time: Use the following to clarify the time relationship between clauses: *after, as soon as, before, when, while, until, whenever, as, once.*	Chaplin was 77 years old **when** he produced his last film in 1966.

Notes

1. Writers may also use *because of* to state a reason or cause. Note that *because of* requires a noun after it, and creates an adverb phrase rather than a clause.

    The conference was cancelled **because the weather was bad**.

    The conference was cancelled **because of the weather**.

2. *Despite* and *in spite of* are also used to show concession. To create an adverb phrase use *despite / in spite of* + noun phrase.

    Despite the full moon, it was very dark outside due to the clouds.

    In spite of the full moon, it was very dark outside due to the clouds.

3. Reduced adverb clauses tend to sound more formal than clauses that are not reduced, which makes them a better fit for academic writing.

ACTIVITY 3

Underline the subordinating conjunction that best fits each sentence.

1. (*Though / Because*) some readers may not appreciate Edgar Allan Poe's dark topics, they are still likely to say that Poe contributed to American literature.
2. Many owls are nocturnal, meaning they sleep during the day and are active (*since / after*) the sun goes down.
3. (*When / Although*) a bank is profitable, it means its financial health is probably stronger than banks with less profitability.
4. One model relied largely on physical evidence (*because / whereas*) the other model focused more on psychological evidence.
5. (*While / Though*) fighting the War of 1812, Britain lost approximately 1,600 soldiers in battle.
6. (*When / While*) not guaranteeing a large salary, a university degree does help new graduates secure a full-time job.
7. People began immigrating to Europe (*so that / when*) conditions in their own country deteriorated.
8. William Ewart Gladstone became prime minister for the second time (*because / after*) beating Benjamin Disraeli in the British general election on April 18, 1880.
9. (*In order to / Because*) meet the new product manufacturing deadline, managers have hired additional contract workers.
10. (*Once / Although*) the city added a new tax on high-sugar drinks, the sales of those drinks started to decrease slightly.

ACTIVITY 4

Read the following paragraph. Underline the five adverb clauses. Then identify the two clauses that can be reduced and write the reduced clause sentences on the lines below.

Building the White House

In 1791, George Washington, the first president of the United States, chose the site for the White House. Construction began in 1792 after Irish-born architect James Hoban won a design competition. It took eight years to build the White House. Even though the White House was not completely finished, it served as a residence for John and Abigail Adams. Unfortunately, the British burned it down in 1814. Soon after, James Hoban was selected to rebuild the house. It was James Monroe who moved into the rebuilt house in 1817. In 1824, while Monroe was living there, he added the South Portico. Andrew Jackson oversaw the North Portico addition in 1829. During the 19th century, people proposed making the house larger or building a separate residence so that the president had more space to live in. Those plans never came to fruition. Since then, the house has been renovated twice. The first time was by Theodore Roosevelt in 1902. He moved the president's offices from the living quarters to what is now known as the West Wing. Harry Truman renovated the White House again because it needed structural work. No other major work has been done since the Truman family moved back into the house in 1952.

1. ____

2. ____

Common Errors

Common Error 11.1 Do you have the correct subordinating conjunction?

because
Communication failures sometimes happen ~~although~~ people misunderstand the goals of the meeting.

REMEMBER: Subordinating conjunctions carry meaning; choose the subordinating conjunction that accurately conveys the relationship between the two parts of the sentence.

ACTIVITY 5 **Common Error 11.1**

Underline the correct subordinating conjunctions in parentheses.

1. The facilitator planned on groups of two to five members (*because / though*) he felt it would offer everyone an opportunity to talk. (*After / Although*) some group members were introverted, the small-group structure allowed them to offer their opinions (*since / although*) they felt more comfortable.

2. (*While / Because*) this experiment might take longer, it is unlikely that the end result will be drastically different (*though / because*) all components have the same chemical base.

3. The presentation needed to be changed and these changes became abundantly clear (*when / although*) the marketing manager looked at the PowerPoint slides. Fortunately, there was time and the slides were changed (*after / before*) they were used at the company's annual retreat.

4. The memoir was not published (*after / until*) 1872, which was 10 years after the artist's death. (*Before / When*) published, the memoir became a best-seller and the price of the artist's paintings soared (*so that / even though*) he never sold one while he was alive.

5. (*Once / Whereas*) the candidate realized he was going to lose the election, he called his opponent and conceded. His opponent changed history by asking the competitor to serve in his cabinet (*as soon as / so*) the election results were final.

6. Traditional English teachers include literature as part of the curriculum (*while / as*) it is a good way to teach character development and dialogue.

Common Error 11.2 Do you have a subordinating conjunction?

When the
~~The~~ student is immersed in the second language, he or she learns more quickly.

REMEMBER: You cannot connect two independent clauses with a comma. Without a conjunction, you have a comma splice error.

ACTIVITY 6 Common Error 11.2

Add a subordinating conjunction to the beginning of each sentence. Make sure to choose the subordinating conjunction with the correct meaning. More than one answer may be possible.

1. ____________ Barack Obama had no military service, he was elected president.

2. ____________ Steve Jobs died, Tim Cook began running the company.

3. ____________ some believe Pope Gregory I was a composer, this has been proven to be an exaggeration.

4. ____________ the first airplane was made of wood, airplanes today are made of metal.

5. ____________ a large portion of peppermint is menthol, it has other content as well, such as menthone and menthyl acetate.

6. ____________ the first electric streetlight was installed in Wabash, Indiana, it became the first city in the world to be electrically lit.

Common Error 11.3 Is the punctuation correct?

The company eventually succeeded~~, because~~ *because* it had a strong product and a smart CEO.

Though many think dinosaurs are ~~dead~~ *dead,* some scientists believe that birds are *feathered dinosaurs* and thereby not really extinct at all.

REMEMBER:
- Do not put a comma before the subordinating conjunction when it is in the middle of a sentence.
- Use a comma after an adverb clause that begins a sentence.

ACTIVITY 7 Common Error 11.3

Read the following sentences. Underline the adverb clause in each sentence. If the punctuation is correct, write *C* on the line in front of the sentence. If the punctuation is wrong, write *X* on the line. Then correct the sentences.

________ **1.** There are sometimes deaths after a tornado, because people do not receive enough warning.

________ **2.** Although it takes a very long time there is an antibiotic treatment that can cure most cases of tuberculosis.

________ **3.** Some people believe wireless performance will get worse because more devices are competing for the same bandwidth.

_______ **4.** She took a course in marketing, so she could add it to her resume and look more appealing to prospective employers.

_______ **5.** Because they had more troops, one country easily won the hard-fought battle.

_______ **6.** He decided a heavy tax on imports was necessary since it was the only solution to the country's economic troubles.

_______ **7.** Although tanning salons have been deemed dangerous many people still tan.

_______ **8.** Since it has small classes and stellar professors, Harvard often ranks very high on the list of best universities in the United States.

Common Error 11.4 Is the clause reduced correctly?

After the construction was finished, the family moved in.

✗ **After finishing**, the family moved in.

After the family bought the house, they moved in.

✓ **After buying the house**, the family moved in.

REMEMBER: To reduce an adverb clause, the subject of the adverb clause must be the same as the subject of the independent clause.

ACTIVITY 8 Common Error 11.4

Underline the subject in the adverb clause and the subject in the independent clause. Can the adverb clause can be reduced? Write *Y* for *yes* or *N* for *no*. Then reduce the adverb clauses where possible.

1. _______ When Valentine's Day started, it was a ceremonial celebration honoring a saint named Valentinus.
2. _______ Some companies excelled during the economic downturn three years ago while others lost profits and employees.
3. _______ While Mexico is the thirteenth largest independent nation in the world, it ranks only eleventh in the world in terms of population.
4. _______ While the movie was not a big hit, it has won several artistic awards.
5. _______ Since hunting decimates the population of alligators, they were declared an endangered species in 1973.
6. _______ When the next earthquake happens, people might be better prepared based on what was learned after the earthquake in Japan in 2011.

Academic Vocabulary

Words from the Academic Word List (Sublist 7)

confirmed	eliminate	equipment	mode	successive
decades	empirical	isolated	somewhat	transmission

Source: Academic Word List (Coxhead 2000)

ACTIVITY 9 Vocabulary in Academic Writing

Use the academic vocabulary in adverb clauses to complete the sentences.

Subject Area	Example from Academic Writing
Medicine	**1.** Although colds can be spread from person to person quite easily, the ________ of colds and many other diseases could be reduced if more people would wash their hands.
Modern Society	**2.** When e-mail first became popular some three ________ ago, many believed it was just a fad.
Philosophy	**3.** Karl Marx described the ________ of production as the way a society organizes its economic production.
Government	**4.** Because she is against most taxes, our current governor would like to ________ the tax that we currently pay on groceries.
Literature	**5.** Even though the language that the author O. Henry used may seem ________ difficult, his works remain very popular more than a century after his death.
Science	**6.** If these researchers want to convince politicians that global warming is real, they will have to present ________ data instead of just personal observations.
Genetics	**7.** Genetic markers, the sequence of DNA used to identify a chromosome, are passed down through ________ generations.
Political Science	**8.** Because North Korea is one of the most ________ countries in the world, most of its citizens have never spoken with a foreigner.
Economics	**9.** An accurate budget for any project usually includes two huge expenses: personnel and ________.
History	**10.** Before information from multiple explorers ________ that the world was indeed round, it was assumed that the world was flat.

Put It Together

ACTIVITY 10 Review Quiz

Multiple Choice Choose the letter of the correct answer.

1. According to the U.S. Social Security Administration, nearly 10,000 people a day are retiring. This could cause problems ______ there might not be enough people in the workforce to do all the work.

   a. because **b.** although **c.** while **d.** before

2. A residency program after medical school can last three to seven years, ______ a fellowship, which is optional training, consists of one to three years of additional training.

   a. since **b.** while **c.** when **d.** before

3. ______ multivitamins, some people may feel nauseous, especially if the vitamin contains iron or if they are taking it in conjunction with other vitamin supplements.

   a. Taking **b.** After taken **c.**Having took **d.** After taking

4. Once fear interferes with daily life, many doctors ______ a patient may soon have an anxiety attack.

   a. believed **b.** believe **c.** were believing **d.** believes

5. When electric cars ______ more than cars running on gasoline, environmentalists believe there will be a positive impact on air quality.

   a. will sell **b.** sells **c.** sell **d.** sold

Error Correction One of the five underlined words or phrases is not correct. Find the error and correct it. Be prepared to explain your answer.

6. <u>When</u> Henry the VIII was King of England, he <u>play</u> a critical role in the nation's religious history. However, he is <u>more famous because</u> he <u>was</u> married six times. He married his sixth wife <u>after</u> executing his fifth wife only 24 hours earlier.

7. <u>While</u> Siamese fighting fish are very aggressive, it is not recommended <u>that two</u> males be placed in the same aquarium <u>because</u> one might attack the other. Females can be housed together <u>although</u> even that is not recommended <u>since</u> females may attack each other.

8. <u>Since</u> the U.S. vice president's offices are located at the White <u>House, the</u> vice president <u>lives</u> at the U.S. Naval Observatory. The house was built in <u>1893, although</u> it was originally <u>intended to house</u> the superintendent of the Naval Observatory.

A climber views the mountains in Sagarmatha National Park, Nepal, which includes Mt. Everest at 29,029 feet (8,848 meters).

ACTIVITY 11 Building Greater Sentences

Combine these short sentences into one sentence. You can add new words and move words around, but you should not add or omit any ideas. More than one answer is possible, but these sentences require adverb clauses.

1. **a.** Many people want to climb Mount Everest.
   b. It is dangerous to climb it because it is so tall the jet stream can hit it.
   c. It is dangerous because the winds can blow more than 200 miles (322 km) per hour when the weather changes.
   d. People want to climb it because it is the tallest mountain on Earth.

2. **a.** Many people would have given up.
   b. The coach decided to continue.
   c. The coach did this because he believed his players could win the game.
   d. The coach still believed this.

3. **a.** Marketing teams often use the color red.
   b. They do this to promote products.
   c. The color red is commonly associated with energy.
   d. The products are related to physical activity.

ACTIVITY 12 **Steps to Composing**

Read the paragraph. Then follow the directions in the 10 steps to edit the information and composition of the paragraph. Be careful with capitalization and punctuation. Write your revised paragraph on a separate sheet of paper. Check your answers with the class.

DESCRIPTIVE PARAGRAPH

The National Oceanic and Atmospheric Administration (NOAA)

[1] The National Oceanic and Atmospheric Administration (NOAA) manages the National Weather Service and plays an important role. [2] The U.S. government uses the National Weather Service to issue warnings that are related to weather. [3] The National Weather Service provides forecasts for local communities. [4] It also covers regional areas. [5] It also manages emergency alerts for severe weather. [6] Severe weather is storms, tornadoes, hurricanes, and floods. [7] There are other agencies and organizations that depend on the National Weather Service. [8] For example, the aviation industry needs to watch the weather in order to keep passengers on airplanes safe. [9] The National Weather Service uses satellites and historical data to improve its forecasting ability. [10] The weather affects everyone on a daily basis, so the National Weather Service plays a very important role; some people do not realize it.

1. In the first sentence, add the adverb clause *because everyone wants to know what the weather will be like on any given day* to the end of the sentence.
2. In sentence 2, add *to decide when* after *National Weather Service.*
3. In sentence 2, change *that are related to weather* to *weather-related* and insert it before *warnings* so the sentence is more concise and academic.
4. Connect sentences 3 and 4 by using *while* to form an adverb clause.
5. It is not good to repeat the same word too often. Change *also* in sentence 5 to another suitable word and make this the first word in the sentence.
6. In sentence 5, add this adverb clause in the best location: *whenever it arises.*
7. The verb *is* in sentence 6 is a weak verb. Change *is* to another verb with a more concrete meaning.
8. In sentence 7, delete *There are* and edit so that *Other agencies and organizations* is the subject to provide the reader with a concrete subject. Make any other necessary changes.

9. In sentence 8, change *passengers on airplanes safe* to *airplane passengers safe.*

10. In sentence 10, add the subordinating conjunction *even though* in place of the semi-colon to show how the two clauses are related.

ACTIVITY 13 Original Writing

On a separate sheet of paper, write a descriptive paragraph (at least seven sentences) about an important person or service. Use at least one example of an adverb clause and underline it; try to use two if possible.

Here are some examples of how to begin.

- *Deans play an important role at a university since they . . .*
- *Customer service is important to the success of a business because . . .*
- *After seeing how often mathematics is used in daily life, . . .*

Michael Phelps competes in the Men's 100 meter Butterfly Final in the 2016 Olympic Games in Rio de Janeiro, Brazil.

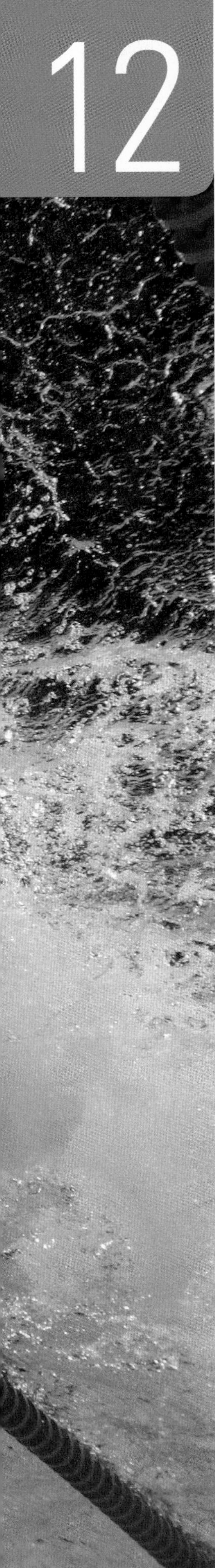

12 Writing with Noun Clauses

WHAT DO YOU KNOW?

DISCUSS Look at the photo and read the caption. Discuss the questions.

1. Do you like to watch the Olympics? Why or why not?
2. What factors do you think are most important for success in competitive sports?

FIND THE ERRORS This paragraph contains two errors with noun clauses. Find the errors and correct them. Explain one error and your correction to a partner.

CAUSE–EFFECT PARAGRAPH

Body Size in Sports

[1] How well do you play a given sport often depends, at least in part, on your body type. [2] Many people believe that Michael Phelps has a perfect body for swimming. [3] At six feet four inches (193 cm), he is tall like many swimmers, but his wingspan—fingertip to fingertip outstretched—is four inches (10 cm) longer than most. [4] Bigger people with longer limbs are often better at swimming and rowing than most people. [5] With larger muscles, they can use more oxygen and so be more powerful. [6] Longer strokes through the water translate to greater efficiency. [7] That you may not know is that bigger bodies are not better for all sports. [8] For example, the best cyclists and long-distance runners are often relatively small and light. [9] Experts suggest this is because the heavier you are, the harder you have to work to move that weight. [10] The best runners often weigh less than 140 pounds (63 kilos). [11] This does not mean that you cannot train for any sport; what it means is that a sport might be easier for some people than others.

Grammar Forms

12.1 Noun Clauses

A noun clause, like all clauses, has a subject and a verb. A noun clause can take the place of a noun in a sentence, so it can be in the subject or object position. In academic writing, the most common position for a noun clause is as a direct object.

Type of Noun Clause	Example
1. *That* noun clause S + V + *that* + S + V *That* noun clauses are formed from statements.	Statement: The earth is getting warmer. Noun clause: Scientists know **that the earth is getting warmer**. (S: the earth; V: is getting)
2. *Wh-* question noun clause *Wh-* noun clauses are formed from *wh-* questions. Use statement word order. **a.** S + V + *wh-* word + S + V **b.** S + V + *wh-* word + V • When the *wh-* word is the subject of a question, the word order stays the same in the noun clause.	Question: How were the banks rescued? Noun clause: The report explains **how the banks were rescued**. (S: the banks; V: were rescued) Question: What happened at the site thousands of years ago? Noun clause: The artifacts detail **what happened at the site thousands of years ago**. (S: what; V: happened)
3. *If / whether* question noun clause S + V + *if / whether* + S + V *If / whether* question noun clauses are formed from *yes / no* questions. Use statement word order.	Question: Was the experiment a success? Noun clause: Zoologists wanted to find out **if the experiment was a success.** (S: experiment; V: was) Question: Did the researcher add the correct chemical? Noun clause: They were not sure **whether the researcher added the correct chemical.** (S: researcher; V: added)

Notes

1. In question noun clauses, do not use an auxiliary form of *do*.
   Yes / No question: Did the researcher add the chemical?
   Noun clause: They were not sure **whether the researcher added the chemical**.
2. When a noun clause is the subject of a sentence, the verb is singular.
   How governments respond to disasters often influences the scale of destruction.
   Whether the discussion would continue was unclear.
3. When a *that* noun clause is an object, *that* can be omitted.
   Scientists know **the earth is getting warmer**.
4. *Wh-* question and *if / whether* noun clauses are also used as objects of prepositions.
   The author spoke about **how he earned his first million dollars.**

12.2 Direct and Indirect Speech

Direct speech means quoted speech, or using the *exact* words of a person or published work. Indirect speech (also called reported speech) means the words are reported, generally using a noun clause. Reporting verbs such as *say, tell, ask,* and *state* are used to introduce direct and indirect speech.

1. Direct speech • Use quotation marks around the speaker's exact words. • Put a comma before the quotation.	The Web site says, "The human population more than doubled during the Industrial Revolution." The reporter asked the candidate, "Do you support an increase in the minimum wage?" The researcher asked herself, "What does this result mean?"
2. Indirect speech • Use statement word order. • Change tenses and pronouns when necessary.	The Web site stated **that the human population (had) more than doubled during the Industrial Revolution**. The reporter asked the candidate **if she supported an increase in the minimum wage.** The researcher asked herself **what that result meant.**

Notes

1. When the quote in direct speech comes first, use a comma instead of a period inside the quotation marks. Do not use a comma if a question mark (?) or exclamation point (!) is used.
   "I have a dream," Martin Luther King, Jr., said in a famous speech.
   "What does this result mean?" the researcher asked herself.
2. For commands, use an infinitive phrase in indirect speech, not a noun clause.
   Command: "Play multiple sports in order to avoid injury."
   Indirect Speech: Doctors tell athletes **to play multiple sports in order to avoid injury.**

12.3 Changing Direct to Indirect Speech

Often the verb form changes in the noun clause when using indirect speech.

Direct Speech	Indirect Speech
Simple Present "Interest rates are stable."	**Simple Past** The news report said **(that) interest rates were stable.**
Present Progressive "We are waiting for aid to arrive."	**Past Progressive** They said (**that) they were waiting for aid to arrive**.
Simple Past, Present Perfect "The grant allowed me to do creative things." "During my lifetime, I have dedicated my life to this struggle of the African people."	**Past Perfect** The writer said (**that) the grant had allowed him to do creative things.** In his speech in 1964, Nelson Mandela said (**that) he had dedicated his life to the struggle of the African people.**

12.3 Changing Direct to Indirect Speech (Continued)

Future	Future in the Past
"I do not believe the world will be wiped out in a war fought with the atomic bomb."	Albert Einstein said **(that) he did not believe the world would be wiped out in a war fought with the atomic bomb**.

Notes

1. The past forms of modals are usually used in indirect speech (e.g., *could, would, might, should, had to*).
2. It is not necessary to change the form of the verb if the situation is still true.
   The teacher told the students that the earth revolves around the sun.

ACTIVITY 1

Read each sentence and underline the noun clause. Write *O* on the line if it is the object of the verb in the main clause; write *S* if it is the subject.

_____ **1.** Studies suggest that low-calorie sweeteners may be just as bad as sugar for controlling weight gain.

_____ **2.** Why ancient people created the Nazca lines in Peru is still not completely understood.

_____ **3.** Have you ever wondered why some people have an accent and others do not?

_____ **4.** DNA results suggest Neanderthals and humans may share some genetic characteristics.

_____ **5.** Ban Ki-moon, the Secretary-General of the United Nations, said that it is important for all of us to do everything we can to secure lasting peace.

_____ **6.** The article suggests that strong government action, along with changes in consumer behavior, could end our reliance on fossil fuels in the next 10 years.

_____ **7.** How infancy varies across cultures around the world is the subject of the documentary *Babies*.

_____ **8.** A thousand years ago, people believed that the earth was flat.

_____ **9.** Whether Shakespeare wrote all of the plays attributed to him has been the subject of much debate.

_____ **10.** Publishers have just announced that Christopher Marlow will be listed as a co-author on Henry VI.

_____ **11.** Some scientists believe there is life on Mars.

_____ **12.** What kind of exercise you do is less important than you think.

Common Uses

12.4 Using Noun Clauses

In academic writing, noun clauses and indirect speech are commonly used:

1. to express the ideas, theories and discoveries of others • Noun clauses are common in introductions, conclusions, and when citing research.	Many people believe **that it is hard to change bad habits**. This, however, is debatable. Matthews argues **that people over the age of 75 should not be allowed to drive**.
2. to paraphrase, which is extremely common in essays that cite research	Although the evidence is not conclusive, recent research suggests **that coffee is good for your health**.
3. to provide more information for a subject, direct object, or object of a preposition	**Why people are moving from the countryside to the city** is the focus of the research. When a teacher engages students, they are more interested in **what the teacher is teaching them**.

ACTIVITY 2

Complete each sentence. Write a noun clause using the sentence or quote in parentheses.

1. (Why are more young adults moving to cities?)

This research paper will discuss ______________________________.

2. (The Arctic polar ice cap is shrinking.)

Climatologists believe ______________________________.

3. (Can we reduce gun violence through tighter restrictions?)

The report did not say definitively ______________________________.

4. ("Absence makes the heart grow fonder.")

People often say ______________________________, but research suggests this is not true.

5. (Reducing food waste may slow climate change.)

The study suggested ______________________________.

6. (How do certain ants become queens?)

Scientists are shedding light on ______________________________.

7. ("We will go to the moon before the end of the 1960s.")

President Kennedy said ______________________________.

8. (Cigarettes cause cancer.)

In the 1960s, doctors learned ______________________________.

Common Errors

Common Error 12.1 Do you need question or statement word order?

Linguists wonder how ~~can we~~ *we can* save dying languages.

REMEMBER: Use statement word order in noun clauses.

ACTIVITY 3 **Common Error 12.1**

Complete the two sentences about each topic. Change the sentences and quotes in parentheses to noun clauses and indirect speech.

1. NASA scientists wanted to know ____________________.

   ("Was there water on Mars?")

   The Mars Rover discovered ____________________.

   (The Plains of Meridiani used to be underwater.)

2. Botanists know ____________________.

   (Trees take up carbon from the atmosphere)

   The botanists found ____________________.

   (Trees trade carbon with other trees through fungi)

3. Researchers wondered ____________________.

   ("What kind of food are consumers buying?")

   New research found ____________________.

   (Consumers buy both healthy options and junk food.)

4. Many proverbs say ____________________.

   (You cannot judge something on its appearance)

   New research suggests ____________________.

   (People are remarkably good at making quick judgments.)

Common Error 12.2 Do you need *that* or *what*?

The paper did not accurately report ~~that~~ what the researchers discovered.

The manufacturer stated ~~what~~ that the problem had been corrected.

REMEMBER:
- Use *that* to introduce a noun clause that is a statement.
- Use *what* to introduce a noun clause that comes from a question. (*What did the researchers discover?*)

ACTIVITY 4 Common Error 12.2

Read each sentence. Underline the correct missing word from the choices in parentheses.

1. Historians are not completely certain (*that / what*) caused the Great Depression.
2. Ancient peoples thought (*that / what*) the sun revolved around the earth.
3. Companies discovered (*that / what*) adding more sugar and salt to food products made them taste better.
4. Biologists have observed (*that / what*) happens to young elephants that have seen their parents killed.
5. (*That / What*) caused the Dancing Plague of 1518 is not known, but about 400 people in Strasbourg danced for days without stopping.
6. This paper will discuss (*that / what*) influences successful weight loss.
7. This research shows (*that / what*) poverty negatively impacts student achievement.
8. The Centers for Disease Control determined (*that / what*) the virus was transmitted by rats.
9. The study looked at (*that / what*) factors increased longevity.
10. Economists worried (*that / what*) the United Kingdom's vote to leave the European Union would affect global markets.

Common Error 12.3 Do the subject and verb agree?

How light pollution affects humans ~~are~~ is the focus of the article.

REMEMBER: Noun clause subjects are singular and take a singular verb.

ACTIVITY 5 Common Error 12.3

For each sentence, write the correct form of the verb in parentheses.

1. What you eat before bed often ____________ (*affect*, simple present) the quality of your sleep.
2. Where sea turtles migrate ____________ (*be*, present perfect) difficult to determine definitively.
3. Researchers found that using a large bottle to feed babies ____________ (*lead*, simple present) to weight gain.
4. How much bosses override their employees' good judgment ____________ (*have*, simple present) an impact on whether or not the employees find work meaningful.
5. What we define as high-speed Internet ____________ (*be*, present perfect) accessible to only 10 percent of Americans, but the FCC hopes to change that.
6. How migrants travel ____________ (*be usually determine*, simple present passive) by whether or not they can get visas.
7. Whether students have a lot of debt upon graduation often ____________ (*dictate*, simple present) their career choices.
8. The study showed that how much fiber people eat ____________ (*impact*, simple present) longevity.

Academic Vocabulary

Reporting Verbs Frequently Used in Academic Writing

argue	deny	find	propose	show
demonstrate	describe	observe	report	suggest

Source: Based on *Academic discourse* (Flowerdew, 2002)

ACTIVITY 6 Vocabulary in Academic Writing

Use the academic vocabulary in the simple present, present perfect, or past to complete the sentences. More than one answer may be possible.

Subject Area	Example from Academic Writing
Health	**1.** Researchers ______________ that older people who exercised had better memories.
Political Science	**2.** President Nixon ______________ that he had done anything wrong, but he was still forced to resign the presidency.
Biology	**3.** Jane Goodall spent many years watching chimpanzees at the Gombe Stream National Park, and ______________ that they exhibited social behavior that is a lot like the behavior of people.
Psychology	**4.** In his book *Awakenings*, Oliver Sacks ______________ the changes that took place when patients were given a medication called L-dopa.
English Composition	**5.** When I was in high school, my English teacher ______________ that I try creative writing, and that changed my life.
Architecture	**6.** Frank Lloyd Wright ______________ that form and function in architecture are one.
Engineering	**7.** The model ______________ how the new electric recharging stations would work.
Environment	**8.** News agencies initially ______________ that more than 10,000 people died in the tsunami on December 26, 2004, but that number rose to 230,000.
Urban Planning	**9.** In contrast to Los Angeles, New York City ______________ a commitment to public transportation.
Performing Arts	**10.** In 2009, in response to an invitation to perform at the White House, Lin-Manuel Miranda ______________ that he create a rap about Alexander Hamilton, which later become the hit musical *Hamilton*.

Put It Together

ACTIVITY 7 Review Quiz

Multiple Choice Choose the letter of the correct answer.

1. The report stated ______ Hispanics are the largest minority.

a. what **b.** that **c.** if **d.** whether

2. We studied ______ happens when you add acid.

a. what **b.** if **c.** that **d.** who

3. President Obama promised that he ______ dependence on Middle Eastern oil in 10 years, but that will not happen.

a. will end **b.** ended **c.** would end **d.** ends

4. The researchers were interested in ______ the rise in water temperatures caused the destruction of coral reefs.

a. did **b.** that **c.** how **d.** what

5. The news report confirmed that the historic sites ______.

a. were destroyed **b.** are destroyed **c.** will be destroyed **d.** had been destroyed

Error Correction One of the five underlined words or phrases is not correct. Find the error and correct it. Be prepared to explain your answer.

6. My experience has shown me what having a positive attitude can help overcome even the most difficult challenges.

7. What the researchers discover surprised the scientific community and encouraged others to try to duplicate their results.

8. People often ask themselves how can they change a bad habit, and recent research suggests some ways this can be done.

Chinese businessmen practice tai chi in a city park in Singapore.

ACTIVITY 8 Building Greater Sentences

Combine these short sentences into one sentence. You can add new words and move words around, but you should not add or omit any ideas. More than one answer is possible, but these sentences require the simple present.

1. **a.** Researchers in England conducted a study on people.
   b. The people lived near more green space.
   c. The researchers found certain results.
   d. The people reported less mental distress.

   ____

   ____

2. **a.** There was a study of more than 6,000 marine fossils.
   b. The fossils were from the Antarctic.
   c. The study shows some facts.
   d. There was a sudden mass extinction event.
   e. It killed the dinosaurs.
   f. It was just as deadly to life in the polar regions.

   ____

   ____

3. **a.** Kenneth Scheve and David Stasavage are professors of political science.
   b. They looked into two questions.
   c. When have countries taxed their wealthiest citizens most heavily?
   d. What societal conditions might have produced those tax rates?

   ____

   ____

ACTIVITY 9 Steps to Composing

Read the paragraph. Then follow the directions in the 10 steps to edit the information and composition of the paragraph. Write your revised paragraph on a separate sheet of paper. Be careful with capitalization and punctuation. Check your answers with the class.

REACTION–RESPONSE PARAGRAPH

Village Dogs

[1] A recent article on village dogs described how these free-ranging dogs were different from pets, working dogs, and wolves. [2] I have seen loose dogs on the streets of many cities, and I always thought that they were abandoned. [3] I learned that most of these dogs have always lived somewhat independently. [4] Research has found that they feed and breed on their own. [5] Research has also found that they take shelter wherever they can. [6] Most of them scavenge for food, often eating garbage. [7] It takes 100 people and their garbage to support seven village dogs. [8] At least that is what recent research suggests. [9] Dogs do not take care of their puppies. [10] I was surprised to learn that fact. [11] After 10 weeks, the pups have to survive on their own, and many do not. [12] The researchers explain that wolves parent in a different way. [13] The researchers say that wolves protect their young and teach them to hunt. [14] Biologists have observed that wolves actually regurgitate food to feed their pups. [15] After reading this article, I think wolves are better parents than village dogs.

1. In sentence 1, change to the present tense to show that the situation is still true.
2. In sentence 2, change the verb in the noun clause to past perfect.
3. Sentence 3 adds contrasting information. Use the transition *however.*
4. Combine sentences 4 and 5 using *and.*
5. Combine sentences 7 and 8. Start with *A recent study suggested.*
6. Combine sentences 9 and 10. Use a noun clause.
7. In sentence 12, change *in a different way* to *differently.*
8. In sentence 13, the phrase *The researchers say that* is too similar to the previous sentence. You can delete it because the reader will assume that this information is from the researchers.

9. For greater variety, change *Biologists have observed that* to *According to biologists* in sentence 14.

10. Change sentence 15. Write a new sentence to express a different idea about the information in the paragraph.

ACTIVITY 10 Original Writing

On a separate sheet of paper, write a paragraph (at least seven sentences) in response to a recent article or book you have read, or a program you have seen. Use at least one example of a noun clause and one example of a reporting verb and underline them; try to use more noun clauses if possible.

Here are some examples of how to begin.

- *The book* Blink *explains why people often form accurate first impressions.*
- *In* An Inconvenient Truth, *Al Gore presents compelling information about climate change.*
- *A recent photograph of ... reveals a great deal about the struggles of people in drought-stricken areas.*

A kea parrot takes flight in New Zealand, showing its brilliant colors under its wing.

13 Writing with Sentence Variety

WHAT DO YOU KNOW?

DISCUSS Look at the photo and read the caption. Discuss the questions.

1. Why do you think birds sometimes have brightly colored feathers?
2. How do birds show intelligence?

FIND THE ERRORS This paragraph contains two errors with different types of sentences. Find the errors and correct them. Explain your corrections to a partner.

COMPARISON PARAGRAPH

Two Smart Birds

[1] Scientists have long recognized the fact that many types of mammals exhibit high levels of intelligence. [2] Including gorillas, chimpanzees, elephants, and dolphins. [3] Recently, however, scientists have discovered just how smart some non-mammal species are, two are birds: the crow and the kea parrot. [4] Clever crows have appeared in stories around the world for centuries. [5] Just like in Aesop's fable, crows will drop solid objects into water to raise the level of the water. [6] Crows can make and use simple tools, like hooks, to get food. [7] Like crows, kea parrots can also use tools, but it is much more difficult for them because of the curved shape of their beaks. [8] While crows are wary of novelty and like to observe their environment before solving a problem, kea parrots are very curious and like a challenge. [9] They will poke and prod something new to try to figure out how it works.

Grammar Forms

13.1 Simple Sentences

A simple sentence contains one independent clause that has a subject and a verb. Possible patterns include:

Clause Pattern	Example
1 subject + 1 verb	Chimpanzees use tools. S V
1 subject + 2 or more verbs	Chimpanzees use tools and can communicate in sign language. S V V
2 or more subjects + 1 verb	Chimpanzees, macaque monkeys, and crows use tools. S S S V
Imperative form of verb	Notice the similarities between the hands. V

Notes

1. A simple sentence has only one clause, which means one subject-verb combination. It can have two subjects or two verbs but only one subject-verb relationship.
2. A simple sentence may have one or more prepositional phrases. Beginning a sentence with a prepositional phrase is common in academic writing.

   In several research studies, chimpanzees used tools **of various types**.

13.2 Compound Sentences

A compound sentence has two independent clauses connected by a coordinating conjunction; the most common are in academic writing *and, but, so.*

and	Zimbabwe was once a colony of the United Kingdom, **and** Algeria was a colony of France. S V CC S V
but	Taking notes helps with comprehension, **but** reviewing notes helps with memory. S V CC S V
so	S. A. Andrée wanted to find the North Pole, **so** he and two others set off in a balloon in 1897. S V CC S V

Notes

1. A compound sentence has two independent clauses, which means there are two subject-verb combinations.
2. Use a comma before the coordinating conjunction in a compound sentence.
3. The most common coordinating conjunctions are *and, but,* and *so.* Other possible coordinating conjunctions are *or, nor, for,* and *yet.*

13.3 Complex Sentences

A complex sentence has an independent clause and a dependent clause. A dependent clause has a subject + verb, but it cannot stand alone as a sentence. It depends on—and must be attached to or within—an independent clause to clarify its meaning. A complex sentence has one or more of these three types of dependent clauses: an adjective clause, an adverb clause, and / or a noun clause.

1. Adjective clauses There are two main types of adjective clauses.	
a. Subject adjective clause: The **relative pronoun** is the subject of the clause.	The Maori, **who** settled in New Zealand about 1000 years ago, are likely of Polynesian descent.
b. Object adjective clause: The **relative pronoun** is the object of the clause. Object relative pronouns are often omitted.	The treaty **(that)** the Maori and British signed in 1840 gave authority over New Zealand to the United Kingdom.
2. Adverb clauses The subordinating conjunction always introduces the dependent clause. An adverb clause may appear either before or after the independent clause.	
a. Independent clause + dependent clause	The average Maori lived to be 30 years old before Captain James Cook visited New Zealand.
b. Dependent clause, + independent clause • In academic writing, complex sentences often begin with a dependent clause.	Although the Maori often struggle in modern society, they have retained much of their cultural heritage.
3. Noun clauses There are three main types of noun clauses.	
a. *That* noun clause S + V + ***that*** + S + V	Researchers found **that** the life expectancy of the Maori dropped after the Europeans settled there.
b. *Wh-* question noun clauses 1. S + V + ***Wh-* word** + S + V	No one is absolutely sure **when** the Maori people first appeared in New Zealand.
2. S + V + ***Wh-* word** + V	Some Maori may wonder **what** would have happened to their population if there had not been European settlers had never arrived.
c. *Yes / No* question noun clauses S + V + ***if / whether*** + S + V	It is not clear **whether** the outcome of the Treaty of Waitangi was what the Maori wanted.

Note
For more information, see Unit 10, Adjective Clauses and Reduced Adjective Clauses; Unit 11, Adverb Clauses and Reduced Adverb Clauses; and Unit 12, Writing with Noun Clauses.

ACTIVITY 1

Read the sentences. Underline the subjects and verbs. Then choose the correct type of sentence. If it is a complex sentence, does it have an adjective, adverb, or noun clause?

1. People in neighborhoods with a lot of trees and grass have fewer chronic health problems.

a. simple **b.** compound **c.** complex

2. When governments improve roads in poor sections of cities, property values go up.

a. simple **b.** compound **c.** complex

3. Although the number of people worldwide has increased dramatically, some countries have a falling population.

a. simple **b.** compound **c.** complex

4. Exercise can strengthen bones, but the effect is actually quite small.

a. simple **b.** compound **c.** complex

5. Because indigenous peoples had no immunity to European diseases, many died.

a. simple **b.** compound **c.** complex

6. Melting polar ice raises sea levels, so many coastal areas are flooding.

a. simple **b.** compound **c.** complex

7. The study reported what the researchers had found.

a. simple **b.** compound **c.** complex

8. The biologists were worried about the population of the eastern lowland gorilla, which lives in the war-torn region.

a. simple **b.** compound **c.** complex

9. The United States government consists of three branches: the executive branch (e.g., the President and Cabinet), the legislative branch (Congress), and the judicial branch (e.g., the Supreme Court).

a. simple **b.** compound **c.** complex

10. After the fall of the Soviet Union, many boundaries in Europe changed dramatically.

a. simple **b.** compound **c.** complex

Common Uses

13.4 Using Simple Sentences

Use a simple sentence when there is a limited amount of information to explain. Simple sentences are used:

1. to state information • In academic writing, this is by far the most common use.	Extreme weather fascinates many people.
2. to give a command or make a request • This type of simple sentence is used in academic writing to direct the reader's actions.	Let's take a look at some examples of this phenomenon.
3. to ask a question • In academic writing, this type of simple sentence is used only once or twice in an essay. It is usually in the introduction to get the reader's attention (called a *hook*) or in the conclusion.	Hook: Why do we call a pineapple and an eggplant by those names? Concluding statement: What will our planet look like a century from now?

Notes

In academic writing, simple sentences rarely begin with the subject. Instead, one or more prepositional phrases appear first.

In this step of the process, the temperature drops.

13.5 Using Compound Sentences

Use a compound sentence when there are two pieces of information to explain. Both pieces are of equal weight. Compound sentences are used:

1. to add information about a topic (*and*) • In academic writing, this is by far the most common use.	Water evaporates from lakes and rivers, and clouds form.
2. to show a difference or contrast (*but*)	Sleet occurs in winter, but hail usually takes place in warmer months.
3. to express the result of information that is in the first clause (*so*)	Colder air is denser than warmer air, so it sinks.

13.6 Using Complex Sentences

Most sentences in academic English have at least one dependent clause. Complex sentences are more common than compound sentences. Complex sentences include:

1. adjective clauses that modify or describe a noun, either by defining which one we are talking about, or by giving additional information	Many of the hurricanes **that form over the Atlantic Ocean** move westward from Africa.
2. adverb clauses that express concession, contrast, result, time relationships, cause or reason, condition, or purpose	A hurricane forms **when the ocean warms during the summer months.**
3. noun clauses that stand in for a noun as a subject, object, or complement in a sentence	Meteorologists explain **that evaporation of water is the first step in hurricane formation.**

ACTIVITY 2

Read the sentences. Write the letter of the purpose of the sentence on the line.

a. to give a command	**e.** to express a time relationship
b. to state information	**f.** to express a reason
c. to add information	**g.** to use a clause to describe a noun
d. to show a contrast	

_______ **1.** Queen Elizabeth, who became queen of England in February of 1952, was crowned in June of 1953.

_______ **2.** Antarctica, which is completely surrounded by the Southern Ocean, is the driest and coldest continent.

_______ **3.** Let the beaker rest for 15 minutes.

_______ **4.** Dogs can see only two colors, but they have extremely sensitive noses.

_______ **5.** A solar eclipse happens when the Moon comes between the Sun and Earth.

_______ **6.** Some students take a gap year because they want to get work experience.

_______ **7.** Jonas Salk developed the first successful vaccine for polio.

ACTIVITY 3

Read the sentences. Combine each set of ideas into one sentence using the connector and the sentence type in parentheses. Be careful with how you sequence the ideas.

1. Bears are moving to places higher up on mountains. Temperatures are warming up. (*so*, compound)

   ____

2. Chile is the largest producer of copper. It is the second largest producer of salmon. (*and*, simple)

   ____

3. The days get shorter. Geese fly south to warmer climates. (*when*, complex)

   ____

4. Cabbage is the main ingredient in kimchi. Kimchi is a Korean specialty. (*which*, complex)

   ____

5. Eva Perón worked to get women the right to vote in Argentina. She was the wife of President Juan Perón. (*who*, complex)

   ____

6. Tennis is played on a court. Baseball is played on a field. (*but*, compound)

   ____

7. More and more people are visiting national parks every year. It is increasingly difficult to have a wilderness experience. (*because*, complex)

   ____

8. An altruistic person sacrifices something. Others benefit. (*so that*, complex)

   ____

Common Errors

Common Error 13.1 Do you have a complete sentence or a fragment?

Emiliano Zapata ^was a leader in the Mexican Revolution. (no verb)

^*He commanded* ~~Commanded~~ the Liberation Army of the South. (no subject)

REMEMBER: A complete sentence must have a subject and a verb. If it does not, it is a fragment. A sentence must include at least one independent clause. If there is only a subordinating conjunction with a dependent clause, it is not a sentence.

ACTIVITY 4 **Common Error 13.1**

Underline the four fragments in the paragraph. Then correct the errors. Answers may vary.

In 1964, Kitty Genovese was murdered in New York City. Reportedly, none of the 38 witnesses called the police or tried to help her. Which was very disturbing to psychologists, among others. Since then, researchers have tried to understand the "bystander effect." In other words, the reluctance of onlookers to take action. Several factors may influence the decision to intervene. First, if there are many people nearby, and no one is doing anything, a bystander is less likely to take action. The fewer people, the greater the likelihood of someone intervening. With fewer people, each witness feels more responsible. Also, people want to behave appropriately and fit in with the people around them. If no one else is taking action, you might think you are mistaken about the situation. In addition, the location may affect whether or not people help. Bystanders are less likely to help in an urban area. More likely to help in areas where people know their neighbors.

Common Error 13.2 Is there a conjunction?

New York style pizza typically has a thin crust, ^but^ pizza crust in Chicago tends to be very thick.

REMEMBER: When a sentence has two or more clauses, there must be a conjunction or sentence-ending punctuation (period or semi-colon). Otherwise it is a comma splice error. A comma is not enough to connect the clauses.

ACTIVITY 5 Common Error 13.2

Read the paragraph below. Correct the five sentence errors by adding a conjunction or a period.

Dystopian literature is a genre in which the author explores social and political issues in a dark and negative future. Dystopian fiction has been around for a while, at least since George Orwell wrote *1984*, it is experiencing a resurgence of popularity, especially among young adults. The *Hunger Games* and the *Divergent* trilogy are examples of novels that have enthralled teenagers as well as adults. Dystopian fiction has a number of common elements, there are usually unjust laws and harsh punishments. The government often uses propaganda it rewrites history. In this genre, human lives are meaningless, mechanized, and restricted. Technology is often misused, people are categorized. Why are these themes so popular? Experts think one reason may be that young people can see how many similar problems the world faces, let's take climate change as an example. It is entirely possible that we will face the kind of devastation depicted in these novels in the near future. Advances in technology may be another reason for anxiety, with devices like smartphones and security cameras that allow us to be tracked all the time.

Common Error 13.2 Does your sentence need a comma?

The whooping crane is still endangered/ although its numbers are increasing. (no comma necessary)

REMEMBER: • Do not use a comma when the independent clause is first.
• When the dependent adverb clause comes before the independent clause, use a comma.

ACTIVITY 6 **Common Error 13.3**

Combine the sentences by using the conjunction in parentheses. Add a comma if necessary and keep the clauses in the same order. Be careful with how you sequence the ideas.

1. A male lion takes over a new tribe. He often kills all the cubs. (*when*)

2. Your cholesterol level is high. You may be at risk for heart disease. (*if*)

3. Two-thirds of both the House and the Senate vote to override the veto. The president's veto of a law stands. (*unless*)

4. A joey, or baby kangaroo, is born. It stays in its mother's pouch for about 190 days. (*after*)

5. The prince can become king. The queen dies, abdicates, or retires. (*only if*)

6. Lausanne is a city of only 146,000 in Switzerland. It is the home to many international sports organizations. (*although*)

7. Lifelike dolls have become popular among middle-class, middle-aged adults in Thailand. Thai people think the dolls bring good fortune. (*because*)

8. In the U.S. Senate, there are two senators from each state. In the U.S. House of Representatives, the number of representatives depends on the state's population. (*whereas*)

Academic Vocabulary

Words Frequently Used in Academic Writing

advocate	eliminate	infrastructure	priority	restore
ambiguous	fluctuations	intervention	random	voluntary

Source: Corpus of Contemporary American English (Davies 2008–)

ACTIVITY 7 Vocabulary in Academic Writing

Use the academic vocabulary words to complete the sentences.

Subject Area	Example from Academic Writing
Social Psychology	**1.** When rules are not clear, research suggests that people are more likely to cheat in these __________ situations.
Government	**2.** Military service should be __________ as it is in the United States, rather than mandatory as in countries such as Israel, Austria, and Belarus.
Criminal Justice	**3.** Without __________, many adolescents with behavioral problems will become law-breaking adults.
Economy	**4.** In the coming year, several struggling high-tech companies announced plans to __________ jobs.
International Business	**5.** India's government recently promised to improve __________ to facilitate growth by spending $11 billion on projects including roads and railways.
Biology	**6.** Evolutionary changes often occur because of __________ gene mutations, such as one 600 million years ago that caused a new protein function, leading to the development of organisms larger than one cell.
Architecture	**7.** Some architects do more than simply design buildings—they also __________ for related issues such as green buildings and preservation.
Health	**8.** According to the World Health Organization (WHO), greater life expectancies worldwide require that every country make healthy aging a global __________ .
Ecology	**9.** Overfishing of larger fish like cod can cause __________ in the entire aquatic ecosystem, making it less stable.
Art	**10.** When artists __________ aging works of art, they often use high-tech tools, such as lasers and other imaging devices, to help them see fine details.

Put It Together

ACTIVITY 8 Review Quiz

Multiple Choice Choose the letter of the correct answer. If no word is necessary, choose Ø.

1. ______ most of Greenland is covered by an ice sheet, its population is confined to the coastline.

   a. Because **b.** But **c.** Although **d.** Ø

2. Buffalo are native to Africa and Asia, ______ bison are found in North America.

   a. so **b.** when **c.** while **d.** Ø

3. Marta, who goes by a single name like many male players, ______ is one of the best female soccer players in the world.

   a. because **b.** whereas **c.** and **d.** Ø

4. Scientists argue that race is a social construct ______ racial categories should be discontinued.

   a. and **b.** because **c.** although **d.** Ø

5. ______ we reduce pollution in our oceans, coral reefs will continue to die.

   a. unless **b.** so **c.** while **d.** Ø

Error Correction One of the five underlined words or phrases (including punctuation) is not correct. Find the error and correct it. Be prepared to explain your answer.

6. Astronomers travel to the Canary Islands with their powerful telescopes <u>because is one</u> of the best places in the world <u>to view</u> the night sky. The Canary Islands have a Starlight <u>Reserve, a place</u> where darkness is <u>protected so that</u> light pollution does <u>not obscure</u> the stars.

7. People <u>can arrive at solutions</u> to difficult problems through a deliberate, step-by-step analytical <u>process. Or through</u> insight. With insight, a <u>solution appears</u> suddenly. <u>Recent research suggests</u> that those sudden solutions <u>are surprisingly accurate</u>.

8. Although one day soon <u>we may have</u> completely driverless <u>cars in the meantime</u>, cars are gradually taking <u>over some</u> driving functions. For example, <u>some cars slow down</u> automatically to prevent an <u>accident, and</u> others warn drivers who are getting sleepy.

A wildlife rehabilitator works with Kola, a western lowland gorilla at the Léfini Faunal Reserve, Republic of the Congo.

ACTIVITY 9 Building Greater Sentences

Combine these short sentences into one sentence. You can add new words and move words around, but you should not add or omit any ideas. More than one answer is possible.

1. **a.** A chimpanzee gazes at a piece of fruit.
   b. A silverback gorilla beats his chest to warn off a male.
   c. The male is approaching.
   d. It is hard not to see a bit of ourselves in those behaviors.
   e. It is hard not to imagine what the animals might be thinking.

   ____

   ____

2. **a.** Some photos are taken by amateurs.
   b. They sometimes acquire new value because of their uniqueness.
   c. They sometimes acquire new value because of their age.
   d. They sometimes acquire new value because of the knowledge that they were once meaningful to someone.

   ____

   ____

3. **a.** Thousands of individuals pass on beliefs.
   b. They also pass on stories.
   c. These beliefs and stories are important factors.
   d. They may be the main factors in determining big shifts in the economy.

   ____

   ____

ACTIVITY 10 Steps to Composing

Read the paragraph. Then follow the directions in the 10 steps to edit the information and composition of the paragraph. Write your revised paragraph on a separate sheet of paper. Be careful with capitalization and punctuation. Check your answers with the class.

COMPARISON PARAGRAPH

Neanderthals versus Modern Humans

[1] Since the mid-nineteenth century, scientists have known about the ancient people called Neanderthals. [2] Like modern humans, Neanderthals originated in Africa, but they made their way to cold and snowy Eurasia much earlier than modern humans. [3] Neanderthals developed differently. [4] This may have been because of the climate. [5] They were shorter and stockier. [6] They had flaring chests and hips. [7] They had prominent brows, wide noses, and sturdy fingers and toes. [8] However, like modern humans, it seems Neanderthals lived in families and took care of their sick and elderly. [9] Recent research suggests Neanderthals also divided labor according to gender. [10] The women were responsible for clothing. [11] The men were responsible for tools. [12] Neanderthals shared so many characteristics with modern humans. [13] Why did they become extinct? [14] One possible answer is diet because perhaps 80 percent of the Neanderthal diet consisted of large animals like mammoths and rhinoceroses. [15] During the Ice Age, they had little access to fat and carbohydrates. [16] A high protein diet causes the liver and kidneys to become larger. [17] This could account for the wide chests and hips of the Neanderthals. [18] When the large animals died out, perhaps the Neanderthals died out, too.

1. To create a little more sentence variety, break sentence 2 into two separate simple sentences. Start the second sentence with *However, they.* joined with *Unlike humans.*
2. Combine sentences 3 and 4 into one sentence.
3. Combine sentences 5, 6, and 7 into one sentence. Use parallel structure as much as possible.
4. In sentence 8, avoid using *like* again to make a comparison. Use *as with.*
5. Combine sentences 10 and 11. Remove all unnecessary words.

6. Combine your new sentence from step 5 with sentence 9. Use the preposition *with*. Remove all unnecessary words.
7. Combine sentences 12 and 13 with *if*.
8. For greater sentence variety, divide sentence 14 into two simple sentences.
9. Combine sentences 16 and 17. Use a reduction.
10. In sentence 18, replace the second *died out* with *did*.

ACTIVITY 11 Original Writing

On a separate sheet of paper, write a paragraph (at least seven sentences) to compare and contrast two things (for example, animals, countries, genres of music). Use at least two examples of each type of sentence: simple, compound, and complex.

Here are some examples of how to begin.

African and Asian elephants share many qualities, but there are key differences.

Short stories differ from novels in important ways.

Although Belgium is a single country, it is home to two major ethnic and language groups, the Flemish and the Walloons.

Steam and smoke rise from the chimneys and cooling towers of a power plant in Georgia, the United States.

14 Using the Conditional

WHAT DO YOU KNOW?

DISCUSS Look at the photo and read the caption. Discuss the questions.

1. What is the function of power plants? What sources of energy do they use?
2. If you were a government official with an unlimited budget, what are two things that you would do to help reduce the amount of garbage that people create every year in your country?

FIND THE ERRORS This paragraph contains two errors with the conditional. Find the errors and correct them. Explain your corrections to a partner.

CAUSE–EFFECT PARAGRAPH

From Garbage to Energy

[1] The United States Environmental Protection Agency estimates that Americans created 254 million pounds (115 million kilos) of garbage in 2013. [2] This fact raises an interesting question: What happens if we invented a process for converting some or all of that garbage into energy? [3] That is precisely the possibility that a group of American scientists at the Ames Laboratory in Iowa is exploring. [4] The idea is to use simple yet modern manufacturing techniques to extract clean energy from the garbage at its source, that is, right next to a landfill or factory. [5] As Cynthia Jenks, one of the Ames Laboratory scientists, said, "Where there is waste, there is energy." [6] It is estimated that converting garbage into fuel and other useful products could reduce U.S. oil use by 40 percent. [7] If the process will be successful, it will significantly reduce pollution and also provide a boost to the U.S. economy.

Grammar Forms

14.1 Real Conditionals

A real conditional clause is a dependent adverb clause (often an *if*-clause) that expresses a real or possible condition. The independent clause expresses the real or possible result of that condition. The following are patterns of real conditionals.

Conditional Pattern	Example
1. present real / past real *If* + S + present, S + present. *If* + S + past, S + past.	If water **reaches** 32 degrees Fahrenheit (0 degrees Celsius), it **freezes**. If the suspects **passed** the lie detector test, the detectives **did not question** them further.
2. future real *If* + S + present, S + future.	If the polar ice caps **melt**, animals like polar bears **will have** nowhere to live.

Notes

1. The conditional clause, like all adverb clauses, can come before or after the main clause, but in academic writing, adverb clauses often begin sentences. When the dependent *if*-clause or any adverb clause begins a sentence, be sure to use a comma after it. Do not use a comma if it comes second.
   Water freezes if it reaches 32 degrees Fahrenheit (0 degrees Celsius).
2. *When* or *whenever* is often used instead of *if* in real conditionals.
   When the polar ice cap melts, polar bears will have nowhere to live.
3. Present forms of the verb in either clause can be present simple, present continuous, or present perfect. Modals may also be used with present meaning.
   If the buzzer **has beeped**, the device is ready.
4. Modals *could / may / might* can be used for future as well as standard future forms.
   If the polar ice caps melt, animals like polar bears **will have** nowhere to live.
   If the polar ice caps melt, animals like polar bears **may have** nowhere to live.
5. Conditional sentences can also use passive voice.
   If the candidate **is elected**, more conservative laws **will be enacted**.

14.2 Unreal Conditionals

Unreal conditional clauses are dependent adverb clauses (often an *if*-clause) that express an unreal or impossible condition. The independent clause expresses the imagined result. The following are patterns of unreal conditionals.

Conditional Pattern	Example
1. present unreal / future unreal • *If* + S + past, S + *would / could / might* + V. • The verb form is in the past, but the meaning is about the present or future. • When *be* is the *if*-clause, *were* is often used for singular and plural subjects.	PRESENT: If the countries **were** at peace, aid workers **could help** the injured children. FUTURE: If the academic conference **were** cheaper, more graduate students **would attend**.
2. past unreal *If* + S + past perfect, S + *would / could / might have* + past participle.	If an asteroid **had not struck** the earth, dinosaurs probably **would not have become** extinct.

Note
Remember not to use a comma when the dependent *if*-clause comes second.

ACTIVITY 1

In each clause, label the subject with *S* and underline the verb. Then write the type of conditional sentence on the line: *Present, Past, or Future Real; Present, Future,* or *Past Unreal.*

1. If the U.S. president does not like a bill passed by Congress, he or she can veto it. ______
2. Many more students would attend college if tuition were free. ______
3. If two parents have blue eyes, it is possible for them to have a brown-eyed child, though this is rare. ______
4. If the composer Franz Schubert had not died in 1828 at age 31, he might have finished his eighth symphony. ______
5. Solar panels do not work when clouds are covering the sun. ______
6. Galveston, an island-city off the Texas coast, is connected to the mainland by a long bridge. If the bridge did not exist, residents would have no way of traveling to and from the mainland. ______
7. In his novel *Fatherland*, Robert Harris explores how history would have been different if Adolf Hitler had successfully invaded Russia in 1942. ______
8. If Peru's Quelccaya glacier continues to melt at the current rate, it will be gone by 2100, and thousands of people will lose their only source of electric power. ______

Common Uses

14.3 Using Conditionals

Conditional forms are common in a variety of academic writing genres, such as cause–effect, persuasive, compare–contrast, and reaction. The conditional is used:

1. to talk about events that are factual or unchanging (Present real) • especially common in scientific writing	If a shark loses a tooth, it quickly grows a new one.
2. to describe routine events that tend to occur at the same time (Present real) • common in social sciences or economics related writing	If a business charges 3 percent extra to use a credit card, many tourists choose to pay with cash instead of their card.
3. to express future possibility based on various possible conditions; the modals *will, may, might, could,* and *can* indicate the degree of certainty (Future real) • common in social sciences or economics related writing	If the supply of gasoline goes down, the price will go up. If the supply of gasoline goes down, the price may go up.
4. to describe a present situation that is imaginary or not real to make a point or, perhaps, a suggestion (Present / Future unreal)	If California were an independent country, its economy would be larger than that of Brazil or Italy.
5. to describe a past situation which did not happen and a possible conditional result (Past unreal) • not very common in academic writing	If Abraham Lincoln had lived, he probably would have fought to get full voting rights for freed slaves.

Notes

1. In academic writing, *if*-clauses (and all dependent clauses) often begin a sentence. A comma is used after an opening *if*-clause.
2. In present and future real conditionals, *unless* is sometimes used instead of *if unless* means *if not.*
   Unless the price of gasoline goes down, some people may be forced to take the bus.
3. Passive conditional sentences are common, especially in scientific writing.
   Some medicines lose their effectiveness if they **are taken** with grapefruit juice.

ACTIVITY 2

Read each sentence and choose the letter that matches the meaning of each sentence.

1. If we do not take steps to conserve or create water, one-fifth of the world's countries will face a water shortage by 2040.
   a. describes a present situation that is imaginary
   b. talks about events that are true and unchanging
   c. expresses the future result of a current situation

2. Newer cars have features to help drivers avoid collisions. For example, if a driver who is backing up gets too close to another car or a stationary object such as a tree, a warning signal sounds.
   a. expresses the future result of a current situation
   b. describes routine events that tend to occur at the same time
   c. describes a present situation that is imaginary

3. Some scholars speculate that World War II might have ended sooner if Germany had attempted to invade England by sea.
   a. describes a present situation that is imaginary
   b. describes a past situation which did not happen and a possible conditional result
   c. describes routine events that tend to occur at the same time

4. Some research suggests that if middle and high school classes began one hour later each day, fewer students would be absent and test scores would improve.
   a. talks about an event that is true and unchanging
   b. expresses the future result of a current situation
   c. describes a present or future situation that is imaginary

5. If people are forced to stand too close together—while waiting in line, for example—they often engage in "distancing" behaviors such as looking at their watches.
   a. describes routine events that tend to occur at the same time
   b. describes a present situation that is imaginary
   c. expresses the future result of a current situation

6. If the United States abolished the income tax, the government would need to find alternative ways to finance its activities.
   a. describes a present situation that is imaginary
   b. describes a past situation which did not happen and a possible conditional result
   c. talks about an event that is true and unchanging

7. Most hospital-acquired infections could be eliminated if hospitals consistently followed infection-control procedures.
   a. expresses the future result of a current situation
   b. describes routine events that tend to occur at the same time
   c. describes a present situation that is imaginary

8. Movie theaters could become obsolete if television quality continues to improve and the price of theater tickets continues to rise.
   a. describes a present situation that is imaginary
   b. expresses the future result of a current situation
   c. describes routine events that tend to occur at the same time

Common Errors

Common Error 14.1 Is the verb form correct for future real conditional?

If the price of electric cars ~~will come~~ *comes* down, more people will buy them.

REMEMBER: Use *will* in the main clause. Use simple present in the *if*-clause.

ACTIVITY 3 Common Error 14.1

Edit the sentences below to insert *will* where correct. Make other changes to verbs as needed.

1. If electronic books continue to grow in popularity, homes of the future no longer need book shelves.
2. If the change is approved by the United Nations, the Czech Republic starts using the shortened name "Czechia" in informal documents.
3. Wushu, a Chinese martial art, is added as an Olympic event if the International Olympic Committee votes to approve it.
4. According to UNESCO, half of the 6,000 languages spoken today disappear if we do not take steps to preserve them.
5. If computer makers are able to develop face-recognition software for cellphones, passwords become obsolete.
6. In the United Kingdom, television owners must buy a license to help pay for programming by the British Broadcast Corporation (BBC). Many people feel this is unfair. However, if the license is abolished, it is unclear how BBC programming is financed.
7. Humans need to find a way to live in space if life on Earth becomes impossible due to war or pollution.
8. Scientists are working on gene-editing technology. HIV, hemophilia, and sickle cell anemia are a few of the deadly diseases that are eliminated if the technology is successful.

Common Error 14.2 Is the verb form correct for present or future unreal conditional?

If humans ~~do not~~ did not know how to sing, they would need to have other ways of expressing their deepest feelings.

REMEMBER:
- Use simple past in the *if*-clause even though the sentence is about the present.
- Use *would* / *could* / *might* + base form in the main clause.

ACTIVITY 4 **Common Error 14.2**

Read each sentence. Underline the correct form of the words in parentheses.

1. Japan (*would not need* / *does not need*) to import oil if it (*would have* / *had*) oil reserves of its own.
2. The rate of global warming (*slowed* / *might slow*) down if we (*will plant* / *planted*) trees instead of cutting them down.
3. A large percentage of medical doctors say they (*did not choose* / *would not choose*) medicine if they (*have* / *had*) the chance to start their professional lives again.
4. If water (*were* / *is*) as expensive as sugary drinks, perhaps consumers (*would be* / *are*) more careful not to waste it.
5. If people (*had understood* / *understood*) the damaging effects of the sun on their skin, perhaps they (*will spend* / *would spend*) less time sunbathing.
6. If gravity (*did not* / *would not*) exist, there (*is not* / *would be no*) force to hold planets in their orbits.
7. If dolphins and chimpanzees (*had had* / *had*) speech organs, (*could they* / *will they*) communicate like humans?
8. Many elderly people say that if they (*had* / *will have*) a chance to live their lives again, they (*would spend* / *would have spent*) more time with their families and less time at work.

Common Error 14.3 Is the verb form correct for past unreal conditional?

If Jonas Salk ~~did not introduce~~ had not introduced a vaccine for polio in 1955, millions of people ~~had died~~ would have died of the disease.

REMEMBER: For past unreal conditional, use past perfect in the *if*-clause. Use *would / could / might* + *have* + past participle in the main clause.

ACTIVITY 5 Common Error 14.3

Complete the sentences to express the past unreal conditional. Fill in the blanks with the correct form of the verbs in parentheses.

1. If Henry Ford ________________ (*not invent*) an inexpensive mass production technique in the 1920s, only rich people ________________ (*be able*) to afford cars.

2. More than 500 people died when the ship *RMS Titanic* hit an iceberg and sank on April 15, 1912. The *Titanic* had lifeboats for only 706 people. If the *Titanic* ________________ (*had*) enough lifeboats, hundreds more people probably ________________ (*survive*).

3. If Isaac Newton ________________ (*not see*) an apple fall straight down from a tree, the scientist ________________ (*might not form*) his theory of gravity.

4. Typhoid is transmitted from person to person. At the beginning of the 20th century, many deaths from the disease ________________ (*could be prevent*) if people ________ (*understand*) the importance of washing their hands.

5. In the 1984 Olympic Games, American runner Mary Decker ________________ (might win) the 3,000-meter race if she ________________ (*not collide*) with another runner, Great Britain's Zola Budd.

6. If they ________________ (*live*) on the same continent, an Egyptian pharaoh ________________ (*could see*) a woolly mammoth. The last mammoths died out about 4,000 years ago, when the pharaohs still ruled.

7. If Brazil ________________ (*be*) colonized by the Spanish instead of the Portuguese, the national language ________________ (*be*) Spanish, like the rest of South America.

8. If the Normans ________________ (*not conquer*) England in 1066, the French language ________________ (*not have*) a major influence on English.

Academic Vocabulary

Words from the Academic Word List (Sublists 9 and 10)

anticipated	coincide	erosion	rigid	undergo
ceases	device	military	route	violation

Source: Academic Word List (Coxhead 2000)

ACTIVITY 6 Vocabulary in Academic Writing

Use the academic vocabulary to complete the sentences.

Subject Area	Example from Academic Writing
Marketing	**1.** The release of the new mobile phone app is timed to __________ with the holiday season. If the app is not released on time, sales will be lost.
History	**2.** If Christopher Columbus had not received the support of the Spanish king and queen in 1492, he would not have been able to finance his westward voyage in search of a new __________ to the West Indies.
Political Science	**3.** According to the CIA World Factbook, 22 of the world's independent countries do not have __________ forces. If these countries were attacked, they would need to rely on larger neighboring countries for protection.
English Composition	**4.** In my view, the European Union needs to __________ a series of procedural and structural changes if it hopes to meet the goal of representing all European citizens equally and democratically.
Agriculture	**5.** In tropical areas, __________ occurs if trees are cut down to make way for agricultural crops.
Architecture	**6.** If a building is made of a __________ material like concrete, and if it is built on soft soil, then it is more likely to fall over in an earthquake.
Weather	**7.** In 1997, if scientists had __________ the effect of the El Niño weather system on world weather patterns, Indonesia and other countries would have had more time to prepare for food shortages.
International Law	**8.** Where will the inhabitants go if an island state such as the Maldives __________ to exist as a result of rising sea levels?
Medicine	**9.** If a __________ that can "smell" certain types of cancer in men passes the trial stage, it could reduce the need for costly surgery.
Intercultural Studies	**10.** Many Americans, for example, feel it is a __________ of their personal space if a stranger stands less than about 2.5 feet (about 76 centimeters) from them.

Put It Together

ACTIVITY 7 Review Quiz

Multiple Choice Choose the letter of the correct answer.

1. If the June 28, 1992, earthquake in Los Angeles ______ during the morning rush hour, many more people would have been injured.

   a. struck **b.** strikes **c.** had struck **d.** will strike

2. Overseas tourism could be hurt if the price of airline tickets continues to rise and more Americans ______ to take their vacations inside the United States.

   a. decide **b.** will decide **c.** have decided **d.** had decided

3. Gray wolves ______ extinct in North America if they had not received government protection.

   a. became **b.** will become **c.** would have become **d.** have become

4. In a democracy, citizens ______ a politician out of office if they are not satisfied with the person's performance.

   a. voted **b.** would have voted **c.** can vote **d.** voting

5. The streetlights in many cities create light pollution so that it is seldom truly dark. If cities installed a different type of streetlight, city residents ______ the stars again.

   a. see **b.** would have seen **c.** saw **d.** could see

Error Correction One of the five underlined words or phrases is not correct. Find the error and correct it. Be prepared to explain your answer.

6. The book *What if* uses physics and mathematics to answer unusual questions related to science, such as "What happens if all the people on Earth jumped in the air at the same time?"

7. By law, the U.S. president must be born in the United States. Thus, Barack Obama could not have become president if he has been born in Africa, as some people have claimed.

8. Opponents argue that if the law were changed to allow 15-year-olds to drive, there would be many more accidents and insurance rates rise for everyone.

ACTIVITY 8 Building Greater Sentences

Combine these short sentences into one sentence. You can add new words and move words around, but you should not add or omit any ideas. More than one answer is possible, but these sentences require the conditional with *if*.

1. **a.** Cows are fed a diet of corn instead of grass.
   b. They grow very quickly.
   c. They can also develop health problems.
   d. The reason is that their stomachs are not designed to digest corn.

2. **a.** Michelangelo finished painting the ceiling of the Sistine Chapel.
   b. After that, he said something.
   c. Michelangelo said, "People don't know how hard I worked to achieve my mastery."
   d. He said, "If they knew, they would not call it genius."

3. **a.** Bees will become extinct.
   b. We will lose all the plants that bees pollinate.
   c. Animals eat those plants.
   d. All the animals will starve.

ACTIVITY 9 Steps to Composing

Read the essay. Then follow the directions in the 10 steps to edit the information and composition of the essay. Write your revised essay on a separate sheet of paper. Be careful with capitalization and punctuation. Check your answers with the class.

CAUSE–EFFECT ESSAY

Save the Bats

[1] Most people have never considered what the world would be like if bats did not exist. [2] My guess is that you have not either. [3] Most people, if they think about bats at all, imagine blood-sucking vampires that spread disease and get caught in people's hair. [4] This fearful image is almost entirely false. [5] It may have come from the fictional story of Dracula.

[6] In reality, bats are gentle creatures that provide critical benefits to humans and the environment. [7] Of the world's 1,000-plus species of bats, only 3 feed on blood. [8] All the remaining species eat insects, fruit, or pollen. [9] One tiny bat can eat up to 1,000 mosquitos in an hour. [10] Collectively, bats eat billions of tons of insects a year. [11] This helps farmers and contributes to human comfort. [12] And plant-eating bats pollinate crops. [13] In tropical areas they spread seeds that help rain forests grow.

[14] At this time many of the world's bat species are endangered. [15] In the United States a condition called white-nose syndrome has reduced bat populations by 50 percent. [16] If bats die out, insect populations will explode. [17] If bats die out, farmers will have to use expensive chemical pesticides to control them. [18] Mosquitos will spread diseases like malaria and bother humans and animals with their bites. [19] The rain forests could die out. [20] We want to prevent this alarming scenario, so we must take action! [21] It is time to commit all our resources to protecting and nurturing our precious friends the bats.

1. Beginning a paragraph with a question is a good way to get readers curious about the topic. Change the first sentence to a question starting with *Have you ever considered...* Replace the final period with a question mark. In sentence 2, delete the word *either*.

2. Change sentence 5 to an adjective clause, and combine sentences 4 and 5.

3. At the end of sentence 7, add *though not human blood* in parentheses. This surprising fact will motivate readers to keep reading.

4. At the end of sentence 9, change the period to an exclamation point for emphasis.

5. To add variety to your sentence structure, change sentence 11 into a compound participial phrase. Attach the phrase at the end of sentence 10. Do not forget to add a comma.

6. It is considered weak style to start a sentence with a conjunction. In sentence 12, change *And* to *Moreover*, and combine sentences 12 and 13.

7. Insert *for example* or a similar phrase in sentence 15, but do not place it at the beginning. Add commas as needed.

8. Too many simple sentences can make your writing sound choppy. Combine sentences 16 and 17 into a compound sentence. Delete the repetition of *If bats die out*.

9. In sentence 18, change *bother* to *torture* to give the sentence more force.

10. Begin sentence 20 with *If* and delete *so*. Exclamation points are rare in academic writing. Change to a period.

ACTIVITY 10 Original Writing

On a separate sheet of paper, write a cause and effect paragraph about a change you would like to see or an action you would like people to take at your school, in your city, in your country, or in the world. Use a conditional in your opening sentence.

Here are some examples of how to begin.

- *Have you ever considered what our world would be like if we used stopped using petroleum?*
- *What would happen if cars were banned in the downtown area?*
- *If I could change one thing about our campus, it would be the parking situation.*

A woman photographs a special display of small books at a book festival in Wales in the United Kingdom.

15 Writing with Connectors

WHAT DO YOU KNOW?

DISCUSS Look at the photo and read the caption. Discuss the questions.

1. What is unique about what this woman is photographing?
2. Do you prefer e-books or print books? Why? What are the benefits of each?

FIND THE ERRORS This paragraph contains two errors with connectors (coordinating conjunctions, subordinating conjunctions, or transitions). Find the errors and correct them. More than one answer is possible. Explain your corrections to a partner.

COMPARISON PARAGRAPH

Print or Electronic Books

[1] As digital books become more popular, people are asking whether print books or digital books are the better choice. [2] Some argue that digital books are the better option. [3] One reason is that an e-reader is easier to carry and holds hundreds of books. [4] Proponents of digital readers also argue that e-books are cheaper in the long run because there are no printing costs. [5] Moreover, supporters of print books disagree. [6] They claim that digital books are more expensive so that an e-reader is a significant investment. [7] Both sides argue that their choice is better for the environment. [8] Proponents of print books say that digital readers do not help the environment. [9] Rather, because technology dates so quickly, old e-readers contribute to the massive amount of e-waste in the world. [10] On the other hand, opponents of print books claim the need for paper for print books will destroy our forests. [11] Individuals need to weigh the pros and cons and make their own decisions.

Grammar Forms

15.1 Connectors

1. **Coordinating conjunctions** connect two independent clauses (e.g., *and, but, so*). • They are usually preceded by a comma. The comma may be omitted if the second sentence is very short.	Studies have shown that the earth's temperature is rising**, but** many people still do not believe it.
2. **Subordinating conjunctions** connect a dependent clause with an independent clause (e.g., *after, although, because*). • When the dependent clause is first, it is followed by a comma. • When the dependent clause is second, there is no comma.	**Even though** the research on global warming is strong**,** some people still do not believe in it. Some people do not believe in global warming **even though** the research on it is strong.
3. **Transitions** are words or phrases that connect ideas in one sentence with ideas in another sentence (e.g., *however, in addition, in conclusion*). A transition can come at the beginning, middle, or sometimes end of a sentence. • When a transition begins a sentence, it is followed by a comma. • When it is within a sentence, it is usually set between commas. • When it is at the end, a comma is before it.	*Beginning:* Einstein won the Nobel Prize for his studies of the photoelectric effect. **However,** he talked about relativity during his acceptance speech. *Middle:* He talked about relativity**, however,** during his acceptance speech. *End:* He talked about relativity during his acceptance speech**, however**.

Notes

1. A transition can also come after a semicolon when connecting two independent clauses.
   Shakespeare wrote 159 poems**; however,** he is better known for his tragic plays.
2. See Appendix 2, Connectors, for a more complete list.

ACTIVITY 1

For each sentence, underline the best connector in parentheses. Pay attention to the punctuation to help you choose.

1. This research paper will discuss why scholars study William Shakespeare, (*and / in addition*) it will discuss his lasting impact on the world of English literature.
2. The computer model indicates the illness should be cured. (*In the same way / Conversely*), tests on human subjects indicate the illness lingers on.
3. Many people make New Year's resolutions to join gyms in January and exercise all year. (*And / Despite this*), 80 percent of people who join a gym in January quit by May.
4. Newspapers are often written in language that is easy to understand, (*so / therefore*) they are usually more accessible than reference books.
5. Engineering fields are growing in popularity (*before / because*) technology growth has resulted in many job opportunities.
6. (*Although / Despite this*) there is no cure for the flu, there are some treatments that can alleviate the symptoms.
7. The large team of graduate students that the chemistry professors assembled allowed them to finish their experiment in less than three months. (*Although / Afterward*), the professors analyzed the results and drew conclusions that will be included in the paper they will present at the next symposium.
8. Many people will still move to California (*yet / even though*) big earthquakes are an imminent danger.

Common Uses

15.2 Using Connectors

Connectors show different relationships between ideas. Using logical connectors effectively will help your ideas flow more smoothly and improve your writing. Be careful, however, not to overuse one or use one incorrectly. The following are examples of some connectors writers use to:

1. give an example Transitions: *for example, to illustrate, specifically, in particular*	Italy has three volcanoes that have erupted in the last 100 years. **For example**, Mount Vesuvius erupted in 1944.
2. add information Coordinating conjunction: *and, nor* Transitions: *in addition, moreover, furthermore*	Mount Vesuvius erupted in 79 CE and buried the city of Pompeii; **in addition**, the small town of Herculaneum was buried.
3. compare Transitions: *similarly, likewise, in the same way*	Pompeii was buried when Mount Vesuvius erupted in 79 CE. **In the same way**, Herculaneum was lost.
4. contrast Coordinating conjunctions: *but, yet* Subordinating conjunctions: *although, though, while* Transitions: *in contrast, however, on the other hand, conversely, instead, on the contrary*	Some people believe a dormant volcano is safe. **On the contrary**, a dormant volcano can erupt again anytime.
5. concede Coordinating conjunction: *yet* Subordinating conjunctions: *although, though, even though* Transitions: *nevertheless, even so, despite this, despite* + noun phrase	**Although** Pompeii was covered in ash from the eruption in 79 CE, the city was discovered relatively intact in 1748.
6. emphasize Transitions: *in fact, actually*	The dust from the volcano could have destroyed the entire city. **In fact**, the ash acted as a preservative.
7. clarify Transitions: *in other words, more simply*	The dust kept the artifacts from being completely destroyed. **In other words**, the dust acted as a preservative.

15.2 Using Connectors (Continued)

8. give a reason or cause Coordinating conjunction: *for* Subordinating conjunctions: *as, because, since*	There are very few digs at Pompeii anymore **because** officials have stopped most excavations.
9. give a result Coordinating conjunction: *so* Transitions: *as a consequence, as a result, consequently, therefore, thus*	Erosion, tourism, and vandalism have all contributed to damage to the site. **As a result**, archaeologists are concerned about conservation.
10. express a time relationship Subordinating conjunctions: *after, as soon as, before, when*, etc. Transitions: *afterward, first, second, next, then*, etc.	Archaeologists discovered skeletons, buildings, and household products **when** excavation started in 1748.
11. give a choice Coordinating conjunction: *or, nor*	The people of Pompeii could flee as the first ash began to fall after the eruption, **or** they could stay behind and hope conditions would not worsen.
12. express a condition Subordinating conjunctions: *if, even if, unless, provided that, when*	More people would have lived **if** they had left Pompeii after the earthquake in 63 CE.
13. express a purpose Subordinating conjunctions: *so that, in order that*	Some Pompeiians went back to their town **so that** they could search for lost relatives.
14. conclude Transitions: *in conclusion, to summarize, as we have seen, in brief, in closing, to sum up, finally*	**In brief**, Pompeii and Mount Vesuvius are topics well worth exploring.

Note
See Appendix 2, Connectors, page 225, for a more complete list.

ACTIVITY 2

For each set of sentences, underline the best connector in parentheses. Then write its purpose on the line.

1. Theft of handheld devices accounted for 50 percent of all robberies in San Francisco in 2012, (*and / or / so*) they accounted for 40 percent of all robberies in New York. ____________

2. A criminal defendant on trial can be found innocent and acquitted. (*Moreover / Nevertheless / However*), the defendant might also be found guilty and be sentenced to prison. ____________

3. The data appeared to support the researcher's hypothesis. (*In fact / In addition / However*), the sample size was small, so some might not believe the conclusion. ____________

4. There are many studies still being conducted on drugs that might cure cancer, (*for / therefore / in fact*) the effects of these drugs on a person's long-term health are still unclear. ____________

5. The report does not mention any evidence of faulty experimental methods by the psychologist who conducted the study, (*meanwhile / nor / but*) does it include any future research plans to try to replicate the experiment to ensure the methods are sound. ____________

6. The initial work on the project was well over budget. (*Subsequently / Consequently / Meanwhile*), the team is no longer confident that the project can be completed with the available funds.

   ____

7. Ebola is a disease that can spread quickly. (*More simply / Conversely / In fact*), in 2014, doctors were fighting an aggressive outbreak of Ebola in several African countries. ____________

8. The data supports the argument that population growth will lead to concerns about water resources. (*Similarly / On the contrary / As a result*), oil and food resources might also be depleted as the population grows. ____________

Common Errors

Common Error 15.1 Do you need a connector?

Plants are essential to life on ~~Earth they~~ Earth because they provide oxygen that humans need to breathe.

REMEMBER: Two clauses in the same sentence need to be joined by a connector. When two independent clauses are joined by only a comma, it is a comma splice sentence.

ACTIVITY 3 Common Error 15.1

The paragraph is missing connectors. Add the connectors, using correct capitalization and punctuation.

but even though since while

Identity theft has become easier, everyone is doing more transactions online rather than in person. People fear identity theft, they are shopping online more than ever before. In fact, 41 percent of Internet users bought something online in 2013. Online shopping varies from country to country. For example, Germany is one country where online shopping is popular. Similarly, China had the most Internet users purchasing a product online in 2015. Online purchases can be from the Web sites of brick-and-mortar companies such as Walmart or Target. The sites of these brick-and-mortar establishments are popular, there are also online-only businesses. Amazon.com is an example. In conclusion, consumers have concerns about identity theft, the benefits of online shopping seem to outweigh the risks.

Common Error 15.2 Is the connector correct?

Plants are essential to life on Earth, ~~so~~ *yet* many tropical forests are being destroyed each year.

REMEMBER: Logical connectors serve a purpose. Choose the connector for the meaning you want to convey.

ACTIVITY 4 Common Error 15.2

Read the following sentences. Underline the connector in each item. If the connector is correct, write *C* on the line in front of the sentence. If the connector is wrong, write *X* on the line. Then write the correct connector above the sentence. More than one answer may be possible.

______ **1.** Today, trash has to travel farther to be dumped in a landfill, so the environment suffers.

______ **2.** A recent article indicates that researchers have developed a new technology that can inject a drug directly into a cancer cell. Similarly, studies are being conducted to determine the best way to treat cancer.

______ **3.** It is important to note how old the buildings in Italy are. Nevertheless, the Coliseum is thousands of years old.

______ **4.** Patients should always check to make sure their medical tests are being conducted at a reliable laboratory. Accuracy of a test method is monitored by the laboratory personnel, whose members should be professionals. However, these professionals should be the ones to conduct the actual lab test.

______ **5.** Meteorologists sometimes study historical patterns to help predict the weather. However, there is no record of a storm as powerful as Hurricane Sandy or Hurricane Katrina ever hitting the United States. Meanwhile, historical patterns cannot always be used to prepare for storms.

______ **6.** One could argue that store-bought vitamins are nonessential and should not be produced. People should get essential vitamins and minerals from food in their diets. On the other hand, store-bought vitamins might be a good idea for people who eat more fast food and have less time to cook healthy meals.

Common Error 15.3 Is a comma needed?

Humans need oxygen to breathe, so plants are essential to life on Earth.

Humans need oxygen to breathe. Therefore, plants are essential to life on Earth.

REMEMBER: Use a comma before a conjunction combining two independent clauses. Use a comma after a transition that starts a sentence.

ACTIVITY 5 Common Error 15.3

Read each set of sentences. Add commas to the sentences where necessary.

1. The American Diabetes Association has more than one million volunteers helping to serve thousands of people who are members of the association. In fact there are more than 441,000 diabetics and their families and caregivers involved.
2. Abraham Lincoln became the president of the United States in 1861 and he issued the Emancipation Proclamation in 1863.
3. Many countries have had female leaders. For example Angela Merkel was the first female chancellor of Germany.
4. An abacus was used by merchants before the modern numeral system was developed. Modern abaci are made from bamboo and use beads sliding on wires but originally they were beans and stones moved in sand.
5. Charles Bridge is Prague's oldest bridge and took many years to build. It was started in 1357 but it was not completed until 1402.
6. A cruise ship is used to take people on vacation and usually returns them to the same port from which they departed. In contrast ocean liners transport passengers from one place to another rather than making round trips.
7. Despite the weather alerts schools decided to hold classes and meetings as if a blizzard were not moving into the area.
8. In conclusion many pros and cons have been presented on the stance of both politicians and readers are urged to weigh them carefully and make choices that are best for their individual circumstances.

Common Error 15.4 Do you have too many connectors?

Because Pluto is quite small, ~~so~~ it was downgraded to a dwarf planet in 2006.

REMEMBER: Use only one connector to express the relationship between two clauses. Do not use two connectors.

ACTIVITY 6 Common Error 15.4

Read the following sentences. Cross out any connector that is not needed. Make any capitalization or punctuation changes needed. More than one answer may be possible.

1. Although some people think driverless cars are inevitable, yet they do not think they should be sold on the mass market.
2. While installing solar panels will eventually save money on heating bills, but the cost is currently prohibitive.
3. Although we have the AMBER Alert (child abduction alert) system, but hundreds of children still disappear every year.
4. While law school in the United States lasts approximately three years, but it takes four years to get the first law degree in Iran.
5. Though an investor may have a million dollars to buy a business, however, that person needs to have additional funds to manage the first year.
6. Because tobacco is a known cause of cancer, so avoiding it might lower the risk of becoming ill.
7. Even though proponents of standardized testing claim the tests are fair and objective, but opponents worry that too much testing results in an overemphasis on test preparation in the classroom.
8. While outsourcing might be cheaper for companies, although the economic benefit is not usually passed on to the workers.

Academic Vocabulary

Words from the Academic Word List (Sublists 8 and 9)

appreciation	crucial	diminished	format	radical
controversy	denote	eventually	portion	widespread

Source: Academic Word List (Coxhead 2000)

ACTIVITY 7 Vocabulary in Academic Writing

Use the academic vocabulary to complete the sentences.

Subject Area	**Example from Academic Writing**
History	**1.** Mary, Queen of Scots, lived a life of ________________. She was forced to abdicate her throne and was later arrested by Queen Elizabeth I.
Political Science	**2.** The Olympic Games have been canceled three times due to war: in 1916, 1940, and 1944. Although the Cold War did not cancel the Olympics in 1980 and 1984, it did lead to ________________ participation when some countries boycotted.
Business	**3.** Experts say that good customer service is ________________ to the success of a company.
Medicine	**4.** Due to the way the airborne disease spread, a ________________ change in the existing protocols was necessary to avoid an epidemic.
Economics	**5.** Many financial advisors believe that everyone needs to invest a ________________ of their money in stocks rather than leaving it all in a bank.
Education	**6.** One way to teach reading is to use a read-aloud ________________. First, the teacher models by reading an excerpt aloud. Then the student reads and tries to mimic the teacher.
English Composition	**7.** Many might be surprised that playwright Arthur Miller won more ________________ critical acclaim for *The Crucible* than for *Death of a Salesman.*
Sociology	**8.** The author notes that social class affects success. In fact, wealthier people are eight times more likely to ________________ graduate from college.
Art History	**9.** Vincent van Gogh is one of the best known artists. However, he died before knowing the ________________ people would have for his paintings.
Mathematics	**10.** The ratio of a circle's circumference to its diameter is approximated as 3.14159. This number is a mathematical constant that mathematicians ________________ with the symbol π.

Put It Together

ACTIVITY 8 Review Quiz

Multiple Choice Choose the letter of the correct answer.

1. When actor John Wayne was in high school, he participated in many other school activities besides theater. ______ he played football and participated in the student government.

   a. For example, **b.** Moreover, **c.** Similarly, **d.** Even so,

2. ______ the loss in funding, the organization did not give up hope that it could continue its research and help improve living conditions for those living in poverty.

   a. Because **b.** Yet **c.** While **d.** Despite

3. The number of technology start-up companies continues to grow in the United States, ______ it is likely that 90 percent of them will fail.

   a. for **b.** so **c.** and **d.** but

4. Homeowners insurance in Florida costs more ______ the strong probability of a hurricane.

   a. for **b.** because of **c.** so **d.** thus

5. The Kodak camera was invented by a man named George Eastman, ______ it went on sale in 1888.

   a. furthermore, **b.** in addition, **c.** and **d.** also,

Error Correction One of the five underlined words or phrases is not correct. Find the error and correct it. Be prepared to explain your answer.

6. Abraham Lincoln, America's 16th president, was best known for ending slavery. Despite his efforts, yet not everyone supported him. He was assassinated at Ford's Theatre on April 14, 1865.

7. Silicon Valley is home to many famous California tech companies. Specifically, the valley is home to Google, Yahoo!, Apple, and Hewlett-Packard. While its fame for tech companies, it is also home to Stanford University.

8. President's Day is an American holiday celebrated in February but the date changes every year because it is celebrated on the third Monday and not on a specific date. In brief, it was created to honor George Washington's birthday.

Rice crops are grown in terraces in Indonesia.

ACTIVITY 9 Building Greater Sentences

Combine these short sentences into one sentence. You can add new words and move words around, but you should not add or omit any ideas. More than one answer is possible, but these sentences require connectors.

1. **a.** There has been a lack of rain.
   b. The crops did not die.
   c. The crops were wheat, rice, and corn.

   ____

   ____

2. **a.** People can determine what their dreams mean.
   b. The article explains that dreams have meanings.
   c. Dreams might be about life or death.

   ____

   ____

3. **a.** Home loans can be short or long.
   b. A shorter home loan will result in high monthly rates.
   c. A longer home loan will lower the monthly payment.

   ____

   ____

ACTIVITY 10 Steps to Composing

Read the paragraph. Then follow the directions in the 10 steps to edit the information and composition of the paragraph. Write your revised paragraph on a separate sheet of paper. Be careful with punctuation and capitalization. Check your answers with the class.

DESCRIPTIVE PARAGRAPH

Monaco

[1] Monaco began as a fortress in 1215. [2] It is located in Western Europe. [3] It borders the Mediterranean Sea. [4] It is the second smallest independent state in the world. [5] It is the smallest country with a coastline. [6] The official language is French. [7] People also speak English, Italian, and Monegasque. [8] Only 37,700 people live in Monaco. [9] According to data from the United Nations, immigrants make up more than 55 percent of the total population. [10] The Grimaldi family took control in 1297 and 1331. [11] The family was not able to secure its rule until 1419. [12] It is now famous for its beautiful scenery. [13] Monaco has low business taxes. [14] It thrives as a place for people to set up new companies and offices. [15] Monaco's reliance on tourism and banking has led to some financial struggles. [16] One time it struggled was during the euro-zone crisis in 2009. [17] Despite this, it is still a much-desired place to live and visit.

1. Combine sentences 2 and 3 with the logical connector *and.*
2. Begin sentence 5 with *Furthermore* to logically connect it to the sentence before it.
3. Begin sentence 7 with an appropriate logical connector.
4. In sentence 9, *make up* is a weak verb. Replace it with a stronger verb.
5. In sentence 10, insert this phrase in the best location to add more clarity to the sentence: *of Monaco.*
6. Begin sentence 11 with the logical connector *Despite this.*
7. Sentence 11 is wordy. Change *was not able to secure* to *did not secure* so it sounds more academic.
8. Connect sentences 13 and 14 with the best coordinating conjunction.
9. Begin sentence 16 with a logical connector that gives an example.
10. In sentence 17, change *despite this* to another logical connector of concession to avoid using the same logical connector too many times.

ACTIVITY 11 Original Writing

On a separate sheet of paper, write a descriptive or comparison paragraph (at least seven sentences) comparing two countries. Use at least one logical connector and underline it; try to use two if possible.

Here are some examples of how to begin.

- *Argentina is located in South America. Similarly, Peru . . .*
- *Despite the fact that Spanish is the official language of both Argentina and Peru . . .*
- *Although both Argentina and Peru border Bolivia, Brazil, and Chile, they each also share a border with three different countries . . .*

APPENDIX 1 Building Greater Sentences

Being a good writer involves many skills, such as being able to write with correct grammar, vary your vocabulary, and state ideas concisely. A good writer also learns to create longer, more detailed sentences from simple ideas. Study the short sentences below.

Jim Thorpe won two medals.

The medals were Olympic medals.

They were gold medals.

He won them in 1912.

He was not allowed to keep the medals.

Notice that every sentence has an important piece of information. A good writer would not write all these sentences separately. Instead, the most important information from each sentence can be used to create one longer, coherent sentence.

Read the sentences again; this time, the important information has been circled.

(Jim Thorpe) won (two medals.)

The medals were (Olympic) medals.

They were (gold) medals.

He won them (in 1912.)

He was (not allowed to keep) the medals.

Here are some strategies for taking the circled information and creating a new sentence.

1. Create time phrases to introduce or end a sentence: in 1912
2. Find the key nouns: Jim Thorpe, medals
3. Find key adjectives: two, Olympic, gold
4. Create noun phrases: two + Olympic + gold + medals
5. Connect main ideas with conjunctions: won medals + but + not allowed to keep them

Now read this improved, longer sentence:

In 1912, Jim Thorpe won two Olympic gold medals, but he was not allowed to keep them.

Here are some additional strategies for building better sentences.

1. Use coordinating conjunctions (*and, but, or, nor, yet, for, so*) to connect related ideas equally.
2. Use subordinating conjunctions, such as *after, while, since,* and *because* to connect related ideas when one idea is more important than the other.
3. Use clauses with relative pronouns, such as *who, which, that,* and *whose* to describe or define a noun or noun phrase.
4. Use pronouns to refer to previously mentioned information.

APPENDIX 2 Connectors

	Coordinating Conjunctions (connect independent clauses)	**Subordinating Conjunctions** (begin dependent clauses)	**Transitions** (usually precede independent clauses)
Examples			For example, In particular, Specifically, To illustrate,
Information	and		Furthermore, In addition, Moreover,
Comparison			In the same way, Likewise, Similarly,
Contrast	but	although while	Conversely, However, In contrast, Instead, On the other hand,
Refutation			On the contrary,
Concession	yet	although even though though	Admittedly, Despite this, Even so, Nevertheless,
Emphasis			Actually, In fact,
Clarification			In other words, In simpler words, More simply,
Reason/Cause	for	because since	
Result	so	so	As a consequence, As a result, Consequently, Therefore, Thus,
Time		after until as when as soon as while before whenever	Afterward, First, Second, Next, Finally, Subsequently, Meanwhile, In the meantime, Then
Condition		even if unless if when provided that	
Purpose		in order that so that	
Choice	or		

APPENDIX 3 Useful Phrases

Contrasting	
S + V. *In contrast,* S + V.	Algeria is a very large country. In contrast, Tunisia is very small.
Contrasted with / In contrast to NOUN, S + V.	In contrast to his earlier works, Goya's Black Paintings were extremely disturbing.
Although / Even though / Though S + V, S + V.	Though London in 1900 was quite different from London in 2000, important similarities existed in population and transportation.
Unlike NOUN, S + V.	Unlike the rest of the world, the United States has not adopted the metric system.
S + V. *However,* S + V.	Single-serving coffee machines are convenient. However, the single-serve packaging is bad for the environment.
On the one hand, S + V. *On the other hand,* S + V.	On the one hand, technology in the classroom can speed up the research process. On the other hand, it can be a distraction.
S + V, *yet* S + V.	People know that eating sweets is not good for their health, yet they continue to consume a great deal of sugar.
NOUN *and* NOUN *are surprisingly different.*	Finland and Iceland are surprisingly different.

Comparing	
NOUN *is* COMPARATIVE ADJECTIVE *than* NOUN.	New York is larger than Rhode Island.
S + V + COMPARATIVE ADVERB *than* NOUN.	Norway extends much farther to the north than Sweden does.
S + V. *In comparison,* S + V.	The average American consumes about 120 kilograms of meat per year. In comparison, the average person in Japan consumes just 46 kilograms.
Although NOUN *and* NOUN *are similar in* NOUN, S + V.	Although France and Spain are similar in size, they are different in many ways.
Upon closer inspection, S + V.	Upon closer inspection, teachers in both schools discovered their students progressed faster when using games.

Comparing (Continued)	
Compared to NOUN, S + V.	Compared to Mexico, Puerto Rico is very densely populated.
NOUN *and* NOUN *are surprisingly similar.*	Birds and reptiles are surprisingly similar.
S + V. *The same* + V.	Brazil was first colonized by Portugal. The same can be said about Canada.
Like NOUN, NOUN *also . . .*	Like Claudius, Caesar Augustus may have also been poisoned by his wife.
Both NOUN *and* NOUN + V.	Both models and real planes have similar controls.
S + V. *Also / Likewise,* S + V.	The new law protects tenants from eviction. Likewise, it protects landlords from tenants who do not pay rent.
S + V. *Similarly,* S + V.	Data from 1990 showed that the number of frogs in the area was starting to increase. Similarly, recent data has confirmed that the population has grown significantly.

Showing Cause and Effect	
Because S + V, S + V.	Because their races are longer, distance runners need to be mentally as well as physically strong.
On account of / As a result of / Because of NOUN, ...	On account of the economic sanctions, the unemployment rate skyrocketed.
NOUN *can cause / trigger* NOUN.	An earthquake can trigger tidal waves.
While S + V, S + V.	While the antibiotics fight the infection, there can be terrible side effects.
S + V. *Therefore, / As a result, / For this reason, / Consequently,* S + V.	Markets fell. Therefore, millions of people lost their life savings.
NOUN *will bring about* NOUN.	New infectious diseases will bring about a need for more affordable treatment.
NOUN *has had a positive / negative effect on* NOUN.	Social media has had both positive and negative effects on reading comprehension.
The correlation ... is clear / evident.	The correlation between smoking and lung cancer is clear.

Stating an Opinion	
Without a doubt, GERUND *is* ADJECTIVE *idea / method / way.*	Without a doubt, walking to work each day is an excellent way to lose weight.
GERUND *should not be allowed.*	Texting in class should not be allowed.
There are many benefits / advantages to NOUN.	There are many benefits to regular meditation.
There are many drawbacks / disadvantages to NOUN.	There are many drawbacks to leaving electronics plugged in overnight.
NOUN *should be required / mandatory.*	Art education should be required of all high school students.
For all of these important reasons, S + V.	For all of these important reasons, the U.S. government should cease production of the penny.
Based on NOUN, S + V.	Based on the facts presented, high-fat foods should be banned from the cafeteria.

Arguing and Persuading	
It is important to remember + NOUN CLAUSE.	It is important to remember that self-diagnosis is rarely accurate.
According to a recent survey, S + V.	According to a recent survey, most people's biggest fear is of making a speech in public.
Even more important, S + V.	Even more important, the printing press made the possibility of self-education a reality for the masses.
Despite this, S + V.	Despite this, most people still lacked the spare time to read.
S + *must / should / ought to*	Researchers must stop unethical animal testing.
For these reasons, S + V.	For these reasons, the Internet should never be governed by one specific country.
Obviously, S + V.	Obviously, citizens will get used to this new law.
Without a doubt, S + V.	Without a doubt, people with pets should not smoke indoors.
I agree that S + V; *however,* S + V.	I agree that a college degree is important; however, getting a practical technical license can also be very useful.

Giving a Counterargument	
Proponents / Opponents may say + NOUN CLAUSE.	Opponents of public television may say that government funds should never be used for entertainment.
On the surface this might seem logical / smart / correct; however, S + V.	On the surface this might seem logical; however, it is not an affordable solution.
S + V; *however, this is not the case.*	Most people believe that biking on the sidewalk is safer than the road; however, this is not the case.
One could argue + NOUN CLAUSE, *but* S + V.	One could argue that working in a start-up company is very exciting, but it can also be more stressful than a job in a large company.
It would be wrong to say + NOUN CLAUSE.	It would be wrong to say that nuclear energy is 100 percent safe.
Some people believe + NOUN CLAUSE.	Some people believe that nuclear energy is the way of the future.
Upon further investigation, S + V.	Upon further investigation, one begins to see why IQ tests are an incomplete measure of intelligence.
S + V. *However, I cannot agree with this idea.*	Some people think logging in our forests should be banned. However, I cannot agree with this idea.
Some people may say (one opinion), *but I believe / think / say* (opposite opinion).	Some people may say that working from home is lonely, but I believe that it is easy, productive, and rewarding.
While NOUN *has its merits,* S + V.	While working at a company has its merits, working from home has many more benefits.
Although it is true + NOUN CLAUSE, S + V.	Although it is true that taking online classes can be convenient, it is difficult for many students to stay on task.

Reacting or Responding	
TITLE *by* AUTHOR *is a / an . . .*	*Harry Potter and the Goblet of Fire* by J.K. Rowling is a turning point for the maturity level of the series.
My first reaction to the scene / news / article was / is NOUN.	My first reaction to the article was fear.
When I read / looked at / thought about NOUN, *I was amazed / shocked / surprised . . .*	When I read the article, I was surprised to learn of his athletic ability.

APPENDIX 4 Irregular Verbs

Base Form	Simple Past	Past Participle
be	was, were	been
beat	beat	beaten
become	became	become
begin	began	begun
bend	bent	bent
bite	bit	bitten
blow	blew	blown
break	broke	broken
bring	brought	brought
build	built	built
buy	bought	bought
catch	caught	caught
choose	chose	chosen
come	came	come
cost	cost	cost
cut	cut	cut
dig	dug	dug
dive	dived, dove	dived
do	did	done
draw	drew	drawn
drink	drank	drunk
drive	drove	driven
eat	ate	eaten
fall	fell	fallen
feed	fed	fed
feel	felt	felt
fight	fought	fought
find	found	found
fit	fit	fit, fitted
fly	flew	flown
forget	forgot	forgotten
forgive	forgave	forgiven
freeze	froze	frozen
get	got	got, gotten
give	gave	given
go	went	gone
grow	grew	grown
hang	hung	hung
have	had	had
hear	heard	heard
hide	hid	hidden
hit	hit	hit
hold	held	held
hurt	hurt	hurt
keep	kept	kept
know	knew	known
lay	laid	laid

Base Form	Simple Past	Past Participle
light	lit, lighted	lit, lighted
lose	lost	lost
make	made	made
mean	meant	meant
meet	met	met
pay	paid	paid
prove	proved	proved, proven
put	put	put
quit	quit	quit
read	read	read
ride	rode	ridden
ring	rang	rung
rise	rose	risen
run	ran	run
say	said	said
seek	sought	sought
sit	sat	sat
sleep	slept	slept
slide	slid	slid
speak	spoke	spoken
spend	spent	spent
spread	spread	spread
stand	stood	stood
steal	stole	stolen
stick	stuck	stuck
strike	struck	struck
swear	swore	sworn
sweep	swept	swept
swim	swam	swum
take	took	taken
teach	taught	taught
tear	tore	torn
tell	told	told
think	thought	thought
throw	threw	thrown
understand	understood	understood
upset	upset	upset
wake	woke	woken
wear	wore	worn
win	won	won
write	wrote	written

APPENDIX 5 Academic Word List

Averil Coxhead (2000)

The following words are on the Academic Word List (AWL). The AWL is a list of the 570 highest-frequency academic word families that regularly appear in academic texts. The AWL was compiled by researcher Averil Coxhead based on her analysis of a 3.5-million-word corpus of academic texts and is reprinted with her permission.

abandon
abstract
academy
access
accommodate
accompany
accumulate
accurate
achieve
acknowledge
acquire
adapt
adequate
adjacent
adjust
administrate
adult
advocate
affect
aggregate
aid
albeit
allocate
alter
alternative
ambiguous
amend
analogy
analyze
annual
anticipate
apparent
append
appreciate
approach
appropriate
approximate
arbitrary
area
aspect
assemble
assess
assign
assist
assume
assure
attach
attain
attitude
attribute
author
authority
automate
available
aware
behalf
benefit
bias
bond
brief
bulk
capable
capacity
category
cease
challenge
channel
chapter
chart
chemical
circumstance
cite
civil
clarify
classic
clause
code
coherent
coincide
collapse
colleague
commence
comment
commission
commit
commodity
communicate
community
compatible
compensate
compile
complement
complex
component
compound
comprehensive
comprise
compute
conceive
concentrate
concept
conclude
concurrent
conduct
confer
confine
confirm
conflict
conform
consent
consequent
considerable
consist
constant
constitute
constrain
construct
consult
consume
contact
contemporary
context
contract
contradict
contrary
contrast
contribute
controversy
convene
converse
convert
convince
cooperate
coordinate
core
corporate
correspond
couple
create
credit
criteria
crucial
culture
currency
cycle
data
debate
decade
decline
deduce
define
definite
demonstrate
denote
deny
depress
derive
design
despite
detect
deviate
device
devote
differentiate
dimension
diminish
discrete
discriminate
displace
display
dispose
distinct
distort
distribute
diverse
document
domain
domestic
dominate
draft
drama
duration
dynamic
economy
edit
element
eliminate
emerge
emphasis
empirical
enable
encounter
energy
enforce
enhance
enormous
ensure
entity
environment
equate
equip
equivalent
erode
error
establish
estate
estimate
ethic
ethnic
evaluate
eventual
evident
evolve
exceed
exclude
exhibit
expand
expert
explicit
exploit
export
expose
external
extract
facilitate
factor
feature
federal
fee
file
final
finance
finite
flexible
fluctuate
focus
format
formula
forthcoming
found
foundation
framework
function
fund
fundamental
furthermore
gender
generate
generation
globe
goal
grade
grant
guarantee
guideline
hence
hierarchy
highlight
hypothesis
identical
identify
ideology
ignorant
illustrate
image

immigrate
impact
implement
implicate
implicit
imply
impose
incentive
incidence
incline
income
incorporate
index
indicate
individual
induce
inevitable
infer
infrastructure
inherent
inhibit
initial
initiate
injure
innovate
input
insert
insight
inspect
instance
institute
instruct
integral
integrate
integrity
intelligent
intense
interact
intermediate
internal
interpret
interval
intervene
intrinsic
invest
investigate
invoke
involve
isolate
issue
item
job
journal
justify
label
labor
layer
lecture
legal
legislate
levy
liberal
license
likewise
link
locate
logic
maintain
major
manipulate
manual
margin
mature
maximize
mechanism
media
mediate
medical
medium
mental
method
migrate
military
minimal
minimize
minimum
ministry
minor
mode
modify
monitor
motive
mutual
negate
network
neutral
nevertheless
nonetheless
norm
normal
notion
notwithstanding
nuclear
objective
obtain
obvious
occupy
occur
odd
offset
ongoing
option
orient
outcome
output
overall
overlap
overseas
panel
paradigm
paragraph
parallel
parameter
participate
partner
passive
perceive
percent
period
persist
perspective
phase
phenomenon
philosophy
physical
plus
policy
portion
pose
positive
potential
practitioner
precede
precise
predict
predominant
preliminary
presume
previous
primary
prime
principal
principle
prior
priority
proceed
process
professional
prohibit
project
promote
proportion
prospect
protocol
psychology
publication
publish
purchase
pursue
qualitative
quote
radical
random
range
ratio
rational
react
recover
refine
regime
region
register
regulate
reinforce
reject
relax
release
relevant
reluctance
rely
remove
require
research
reside
resolve
resource
respond
restore
restrain
restrict
retain
reveal
revenue
reverse
revise
revolution
rigid
role
route
scenario
schedule
scheme
scope
section
sector
secure
seek
select
sequence
series
sex
shift
significant
similar
simulate
site
so-called
sole
somewhat
source
specific
specify
sphere
stable
statistic
status
straightforward
strategy
stress
structure
style
submit
subordinate
subsequent
subsidy
substitute
successor
sufficient
sum
summary
supplement
survey
survive
suspend
sustain
symbol
tape
target
task
team
technical
technique
technology
temporary
tense
terminate
text
theme
theory
thereby
thesis
topic
trace
tradition
transfer
transform
transit
transmit
transport
trend
trigger
ultimate
undergo
underlie
undertake
uniform
unify
unique
utilize
valid
vary
vehicle
version
via
violate
virtual
visible
vision
visual
volume
voluntary
welfare
whereas
whereby
widespread